PRA

Unh

"Getting unstuck (and we're all stuck in something whether we acknowledge it or not) is vital work. And Sunny who actually broke free is the perfect guide. Part memoir, part manual, this book is for anyone who, as Sunny invites, knows they are meant for something more."

> — **PAM GROUT**, #1 *New York Times* bestselling author of 19 books including *E-Squared, Thank & Grow Rich,* and *Art & Soul, Reloaded*

"It's too easy to stay in a toxic relationship because of the myriad fears our minds create around leaving. *Unhitched* doesn't just give us permission to move on from our unhealthy marriages or partnerships, it gives us the tools to do it, with confidence and grace. This is a beautiful book, rich with lessons for living our truest lives. Through relevant stories, insightful writing exercises and a clear wisdom gleaned from a woman who has been there, Sunny Joy McMillan walks us down the necessary path of self-love, so that our decision to leave — or to stay — can be rooted in freedom rather than fear."

> — **SCOTT STABILE**, author of *Big Love: The Power of Living with a Wide-Open Heart*

"Sunny Joy's *Unhitched* beautifully weaves her own larger than life divorce tale (imagine living in Paris Hilton's home, hosting glamorous boozy parties and brunching at The Ivy) with the incredible wisdom that can only come from living one's truth. Wonderful stories of discovery from Sunny's clients bring depth and breadth to this warm guide to forging your ideal relationship. A wonderful read for anyone trying to decide, 'Should I stay or should I go?'"

> — **SARAH BAMFORD SEIDELMANN**, MD, author of *Swimming with Elephants*

Unhitched

UNHITCHED

Unlock Your Courage and Clarity to Unstick Your Bad Marriage

SUNNY JOY MCMILLAN

NEW YORK

LONDON • NASHVILLE • MELBOURNE • VANCOUVER

Unhitched

Unlock Your Courage and Clarity to Unstick Your Bad Marriage

Published in New York, New York, by Morgan James Publishing in partnership with Difference Press. Morgan James is a trademark of Morgan James, LLC. www.MorganJamesPublishing.com

ISBN 9781642790375 paperback
ISBN 9781642790382 eBook
Library of Congress Control Number: 2018938267

Cover Design by:
Megan Dillon
megan@creativeninjadesigns.com

Interior Design by:
Chris Treccani
www.3dogcreative.net

Morgan James is a proud partner of Habitat for Humanity Peninsula and Greater Williamsburg. Partners in building since 2006.

Get involved today! Visit
MorganJamesPublishing.com/giving-back

For all the women who know they are meant for more.

TABLE OF CONTENTS

AUTHOR'S NOTE

*One of my greatest lifelong goals has been to ensure that
absolutely everyone likes me and no one is mad at me – ever.
Unfortunately, my other goal has been to be a writer.*
KELSEY MILLER, *Big Girl*

This book is largely a guide to unsticking a bad, unhappy, or
unfulfilling marriage (whether or not that means divorce).
It includes case studies of awesome clients, as well as personal
stories of important friends and mentors. Unless I have received
express approval from said people to appear as they are in real
life, names have been changed and identifying characteristics
withheld – or at least fiddled with a bit – for purposes of
anonymity.

You might also be wondering how my ex-husband feels
about the book. Fair enough. I've shared some pretty personal
details about our lives and marriage in here. He's actually been
an integral part in the writing of the book, supporting me in
incredible ways and providing a sounding board during times
of self-doubt or stuckness. He remains one of my biggest,
staunchest advocates, and our post-divorce friendship has been
one of the most beautiful gifts I've received in this lifetime. The

levels of honesty, forgiveness, and amends we keep transcending as the years go by continue to blow my mind and heart.

That's actually the reason for this note. I want to give him a say in all this. While this little note is a paltry substitute for actually sharing his side of the story in his own words, it's the best I could come up with to honor his voice in some way.

As much as this book is a guide, you'll also find that it's in part a tiny memoir that tracks my marital journey, from meeting this man who would later become my husband, all the way through our divorce. Due to structure and length, however, this book was not intended to share everything about my life or our marriage. And although the title of this book might suggest that mine was a bad marriage, that's not the full story, and it's not (I think) how my ex-husband would characterize it.

True, it was not all bad. But it certainly was not all good, either. Not all black or all white, but gray and murky, meaning we don't necessarily see eye-to-eye on everything. We're human and our memories are, by definition, selective and fallible. Despite grand efforts to agree on a shared narrative about our relationship, there are gaps in recollected facts and differences of opinion on how things went down – or should have gone down. I'm not sure we'll ever agree on these things. And that's okay.

My intent in this book is to convey what happened between us in a graceful way *based on my point of view*. I can only speak from my experience of it all. I hope upon reading it you feel the love and respect I carry for this man. Nevertheless, I remain resolute and at peace with my decision to unstick our marriage by ending it. My ex-husband, on the contrary, remains resolute that our marriage should not have ended – especially in the way that it did, leaving him wanting certain things from me that I was unwilling to give at the time. It is also safe to say he is far from at peace with the decision.

I think where my ex and I can agree is that ours was a hard marriage. Things were never easy, even in the very beginning of our dating relationship. That conflict took a toll on us both. He weathered it better than I. His preference would have been a continued fight for our marital survival. I, on the other hand, bowed out in search of peace. These are the places where we may never find common ground. And I want to honor those sacred places. I hope I have done so adequately, more than anything, for him.

SUNNY JOY MCMILLAN
Seattle, WA
Jan. 12, 2018

Postscript

Between submitting the final draft of my manuscript for publication and my receipt of a galley copy for review, my amazing ex-husband passed away on June 26, 2018. I decided not to edit the original Author's Note because I shared this version with him in early 2018. Not only did he approve, but I recall he said something along the lines of, "Wow, Sunny, you nailed it." It just seemed appropriate to leave it as-is. I miss you dearly, Rob.

Robert Earl Kientz

(1966 – 2018) – Loved, Honored, and Remembered.

INTRODUCTION

*Many people die at twenty-five and aren't buried
until they are seventy-five.*

BENJAMIN FRANKLIN

Not too long ago, I was listening to an online conference with
a panel of experts presenting on mind, body, and spirit
wellness. From holistic psychiatrists to green juicers to pioneers
in self-compassion research, their theme was connecting
to one's best self. My ears perked up when I heard one of the
speakers mention her research with a palliative care worker
who had served thousands of patients. According to her, the
number one biggest regret of the dying is that they hadn't
lived true to themselves. Instead, they had lived according to
the expectations of others and paid too much attention to the
"shoulds." The speaker felt that these patients had not had
enough trust in who they were to live in alignment with their
heart and spirit.

This evidence is disappointing, especially for those dying
patients. However, it is not surprising to me. I'm a recovering
attorney and a practicing master life coach. One of the biggest
concerns I hear from my clients (and frankly, some colleagues,
as well!) is that they are not living the lives they desire in

accordance with their own personal truth. Up until several years ago, I myself was not living according to the truth of my own being either. I'd spent my first 30-some-odd years creating a perfect-looking life, complete with an incredibly successful attorney husband and a respectable but short-lived career as an attorney myself. After leaving my firm, I channeled my energy into becoming what can best be described as a trophy wife addicted to transforming her appearance into that of Malibu Barbie. Our flashy lifestyle reflected my husband's wild professional success and, from the outside, I imagine it all looked pretty good. At least that was the goal.

Much like the regretful patients above, however, internally I'd been living in complete disconnection from the longings of my own heart and spirit. My marriage was a dysfunctional wreck that was only limping along with the help of crutches like great wealth to keep us distracted, great booze to keep us happily numb, great friends to provide us the intimacy we failed to provide each other – and a great deal of space between us as we lived largely separate lives, thereby minimizing the high level of conflict that had plagued us ever since we met.

Keeping up the illusion of perfection took its toll. I was exhausted and began to recognize that this way of living was not sustainable, even if I'd wanted it to be. But I didn't. I hated that I lived in constant anger at my husband. It just didn't feel like me. Where was the happy-go-lucky girl with a natural set point for peace and contentment? It seemed she was long gone. After years of mutual resentments and fights where lines had been crossed and envelopes pushed to the point of no return, I often found it difficult to look at him without contempt goggles obstructing my view.

It dawned on me that I was angry at him *just for being him,* a realization that came with deep shame and guilt. My husband, while hot-tempered and often difficult, was not an abuser, an addict, or an adulterer. He was a good man. But like oil and water, we just couldn't seem to get along, despite an amazingly comfortable life that should have paved the way for ease and peace.

The dawning recognition that my marriage was not working was coupled with a crippling fear of what it would look like were we to get divorced. Although I had a law degree from a top tier school and a couple of years under my belt as an associate with a well-respected, large, civil defense law firm, I hadn't worked in several years. I also knew (for reasons I will explain later in more detail) that I would not be entitled to the traditional division of assets afforded to spouses in Texas upon divorce. I was too ashamed to admit this to anyone but the mental health professionals we'd seen for couples counseling. I knew if I walked away from my marriage, I'd not only lose my husband, but also the life we had built. And it was an incredibly blessed life for which I was profoundly grateful. I wanted for nothing ... except a functional, loving marriage.

By this time, I was scratching the surface of the world of self-help, previously unknown to me. It would be several years of my own personal work before I'd start a professional career in this field. At the time, however, I knew enough to trust my gut, and I was beginning to suspect that the Universe had my back. I also knew that my husband and I deserved better from each other. Despite years of opportunity, our unkind, combative ways had not changed.

Finally, I reached a point when the pain of staying put exceeded my fear of the unknown. So I leapt, out of my marriage

– directly into the unknown. That leap ultimately landed me here, several years post-divorce, writing this book for you, dear reader. My hope is that through my story, you will feel less alone in yours. And through the sharing of my experience and knowledge, both personal and professional, you will be able to make the right choice for your life and marriage that will be in the highest and best interest of all involved.

When it comes to a relationship as important and widely recognized as marriage, often there will be many well-meaning (and some not-so-well-meaning) voices offering various opinions as to what you should do and how you should proceed. Whether they come from friends, family, or strangers in the supermarket checkout line, you gotta be ready to sift through the noise and tune out any unhelpful or unsolicited advice. These are sacred decisions that belong to you and your spouse (and potentially any children of appropriate age who will be affected). And there are many tools and techniques that can help you make those tough choices, as well as plenty of pitfalls to avoid.

That's where I come in. I am passionately committed to helping my clients get unstuck from bad marriages (although that doesn't necessarily always mean divorce – more on that later, though!). Remaining stagnant in the wrong marriage doesn't do anyone any favors. Remember those regretful, dying patients from the beginning of this chapter? This is not the time to make the same mistake they did and live according to the expectations of others. This *is the time* to live in alignment with your own heart and spirit. By the end of this book, you will have a plan for moving forward in your marriage with courage and clarity. The process outlined in the chapters to follow will guide you to a life aligned with your heart and spirit – a life without the severe regret of not having lived according to your truth.

My wish is for your marriage, and the decisions you make about it, to reflect your deepest truth. My process will help get you there. You've got this. Promise.

CHAPTER 1

Me Too

Take to the streets with our messy, imperfect, wild, stretch-marked, wonderful, heartbreaking, grace-filled, and joyful lives.
BRENÉ BROWN, *The Gifts of Imperfection*

Janie sat down across the table from me at a little coffee shop near my office. A collaborator on a couple of business projects, Janie and I shared many interests and had become fairly close friends. Although I wasn't exactly sure why she'd asked me to meet her that day, I had a hunch. After grabbing a latte and sharing some chitchat, Janie got down to business.

"So ... it's about my marriage," she began, validating my suspicions. For years, I always seemed to be the go-to person when it came to personal confessions among my friends. It was usually relationship-related. I knew which friends had had affairs, which husbands had substance addictions or spent too much time at the local strip club, and which moms were really struggling as new parents. I'm not sure how exactly I ended up in the position of "bearer of marriage secrets," but I loved that my friends felt safe enough to share with me and that they felt no judgment from me when they did. That day with Janie at the coffee shop was no exception. Now, however, I had a professional career in this very area, so the number of people sharing their relationship woes had increased exponentially. There was little that shocked me anymore.

Janie went on to explain that her marriage had not been in a great place for a while. She and her husband were just so different. And, as I hear consistently from so many clients, her own personal transformational work was outpacing her husband's. He just didn't show much interest in growth or spiritual matters, despite her efforts to share her discoveries. Janie felt frustrated and alone. Add to that no sex in months, plus financial power struggles between the two of them, and they just weren't connecting on much of anything. She wasn't sure her marriage was going to survive.

In such situations, it is not my job to tell the friend or client what to do. Instead, I do my best to listen well, ask tough questions, and maybe throw in a few handy coaching tools, all of which are designed to help the person sitting across from me uncover their own truth and decide the best way forward. This book is designed with that exact same intent in mind.

One of the most important things to remember as you are doing this work, dear reader, is that you are not alone. I myself have carried the shame of an unhappy marriage. I would hazard a guess that fellow readers of this book have a few shameful marital secrets of their own. But now it's time to put down the mask and pick up the antidote to shame: shining a light on the dark places of our shared issues, the ones that previously kept us isolated, separate, and hiding.

I see you. And I want you to know that I understand just how exhausting it is to maintain a mask of perfection – always putting up a good front at family gatherings and cocktail parties for fear that others might know your life is not rainbows, unicorns, and perpetual marital bliss. I know what it's like to feel a fight coming on in public, hissing at your husband through clenched teeth and a fake smile to "please keep it down and try to look pleasant – I'd really rather not have a room full of 100 people witness our meltdown." I know the humiliation following a blowup you simply could not suppress, the eyes of onlookers cast down and away out of some mixture of politesse and awkwardness. I know what it's like to sob in a bathroom stall at a restaurant, hoping for enough of a temporary release on the pressure valve of emotion to allow you to make it through the rest of a meal.

You may even have attended couples counseling or pursued your own therapy. Such efforts might have improved the situation a bit ... but somehow your issues continue to follow you. All the while, there is a niggling suspicion buried below the surface that you are in the wrong marriage and this is not your right life. But any acknowledgement of your doubts sends your head spinning off into a future trip of epic proportions, envisioning what your life would even look like were you to leave. Your mind offers up a whole host of concerns, like what will you do for health insurance and can you afford the property taxes if you get the house? You haven't worked in years and have heard the job market is brutal these days – what if your husband's threats that you'll get nothing in a divorce are true and you can't support yourself? What if you never find love again and grow old alone – isn't a passable marriage better than that scary alternative?

At some point, out of sheer exhaustion and fear, you resign yourself to simply staying put. Other than an unhappy marriage, everything else looks pretty darn good – comfortable lifestyle with a nice home, shopping excursions, personal trainers, and regular vacations. And don't forget to add in plenty of women and wine (read: whine) time, where everyone vents, sometimes to the point of a vulnerability hangover, about how annoying / frustrating / oblivious / unhelpful / [insert your own adjective here] their respective husbands are.

So you convince yourself that a tolerable marriage will do just fine. Besides, aren't most of the married people around you repeating that oft-cited cliché that "marriage is hard"? You find some small solace in telling yourself this is just the way of this entrenched institution. It's fairytale nonsense to expect a happy union full of fun, love, and healthy communication. Navel-gazing about the state of your marriage is a First World problem after all, and your life really isn't that bad, is it? Aren't there women in other countries where spousal rape and abuse are legal who aren't even allowed to drive? Surely you can put up with one more year of a loveless marriage when you have other areas of your life from which you can draw fulfillment and joy.

Years pass as you ride this constant seesaw. One day you are resolute that you must go. You are confident that no matter what happens, you will be okay. And frankly, there are those days when your conviction overrides your fear, and you don't give a flying fig if you leave with only the clothes on our back – you know your freedom is worth it.

The next day, the seesaw plummets to the other side, leaving you unsure about your options and future. The voice of doubt convinces you that it's safer to stay put until you know your assets will be more secure or until your kids are [out of diapers

... in middle school ... graduating college]. Or maybe you want him to make the first move – if he had an affair, for example, then you'd have a good enough reason to leave immediately. But for now, you wait. Stagnation interspersed with occasional blips of happiness or pain becomes the norm.

Many women will live a lifetime like this. Till death (emotional first, then physical) them do part. The struggle is real, ladies. All of it. But you know what else is real? Perhaps even more real than the confusion, the fear, and the swirling, conflicted feelings? The still, small voice that has whispered to you, sometimes gently, sometimes firmly, that *you are meant for more*. That marriage doesn't have to be so hard. That you deserve a fulfilling, loving, and kind relationship. That you can trust the vision you've seen in your mind's eye of a bright future. And that you have the power to make it all so.

Just several years ago, I put fear in the backseat and let the still, small voice take the wheel. To date, not once has it led me astray. You, too, can trust the still, small voice, and I'm going to show you how. Ready? Let's go!

CHAPTER 2

My Story

Be brave enough to turn away from shiny objects, and toward
the light that makes them shine.
MARTHA BECK

Off in La-La Land

I pushed through the throngs of people dancing in the living room and waved at the DJ, as I passed by on my way to the kitchen. It was our annual New Year's Eve party at our vacation home in Los Angeles, and the party was in full force. I loved seeing the house so full of happy faces and celebration.

Although we typically had servers to ensure things ran smoothly, I never could relax at these affairs. It always seemed like we were low on ice, and I had to make sure everyone had a cold mixed drink in hand. The more inebriated, the better in my book – the smiles were bigger, the laughter more boisterous, and I could just float in that sea of liquid warmth and fun.

I glanced at the clock. "Crap! It's almost midnight." I looked around furtively for my husband. I couldn't miss another New Year's Eve kiss. For years, it seemed I was always on the hunt for more ice or a drink refill when guests began the countdown, and I inevitably found myself on my own at the stroke of midnight. This always irked my husband. Understandably so. And unfortunately, tonight was no different. Once again, we didn't find each other until after 12 a.m.

By this point in our relationship, I knew my husband's inevitable blowup about the incident revealed an intense hurt at his growing realization that he didn't seem to rank higher than fresh ice in my book. All I could worry about now, though, was smoothing things over so our guests wouldn't witness a fight. I'd learned my lesson about this in year three of our relationship when a conflict had humiliatingly escalated beyond acceptable limits in front of several people. Never again, I had promised myself. I was committed to hiding our marital problems at whatever cost. So when I finally found my husband, I made a most pleading apology, quickly followed by too much explanation, all while swearing it would be different in the future, and then went on about my façade of a merry way. *Now, where was that ice?*

Within several hours, the final guests would be filtering out and heading home or to some after-hour's party farther up in the hills that promised plenty of celebrity sightings. My husband would be long asleep. Save for special occasions like Vegas and New Year's, it was usually a stretch if he made it to midnight, and he'd disappear upstairs soon thereafter. Those who knew us well were familiar with this routine.

In the wee hours of the morning, I padded around the house doing a clean sweep to get things to a passable condition before the cleaning crew arrived the following morning and we headed out to brunch at The Ivy. Often it still amazed me that this was my life, although I couldn't take too much credit for it. Rarely a day went by that I didn't acknowledge with heartfelt gratitude the ridiculously over-the-top lifestyle my husband's work afforded us. Despite our issues, I had to give him credit. From a modest upbringing in the Midwest, he'd gone on to become a chemical engineer, then an attorney who co-founded a law firm that regularly took on some of the largest chemical and pharmaceutical corporations in the world, Erin Brockovich-style. As his firm continued to grow and expanded its reach into new cities, so too did our life. And so too the disconnect between us.

I spent a lot of solo time in those early morning hours after the many parties we threw, from Austin to L.A. The house always felt so still, so empty. I usually found myself exhausted, feet throbbing from hours in stiletto heels, but unable to go to sleep if things were messy. It was in those times, when my buzz was wearing off and my body was spent, that the still, small voice inside me could be heard.

That voice would remind me of the huge disconnect that existed between the happy party face I wore most of the time – and the gaping chasm between my husband and me. I just kept thinking that maybe as he became more successful and kept hitting his self-imposed, ever-rising income thresholds, things would improve. Maybe, like an arranged marriage, we'd grow fond of each other and find a comfortable rhythm in a peaceful coexistence. Maybe the conflict would decrease. Maybe my husband would finally shake his depression, workaholism, and hermitic ways. Maybe I would finally stop seething with anger below my forced perma-smile.

But it had been over a decade, and little had changed. We'd had more marital counseling than I cared to remember. Certainly, it didn't bode well that the months following our honeymoon had found us in extreme couples counseling. I call it extreme because we each had our own therapist, and then would come together as a group of four. Apparently our issues were too big for one psychologist to handle! And although we'd both expressed a desire for children someday, we consciously decided not to have any, at least for the time being. From my perspective, all that fighting and dysfunction was no place for a child. But I began to wonder, if my marriage wasn't good enough for children, how could it be good enough for us? That and so many other questions about my relationship and future ran through my head on a regular basis.

After a weary sigh acknowledging that things weren't likely to change, the guilt and shame would set in. How the heck could I be so ungrateful? Here I was, standing in our West Hollywood vacation home that we'd purchased from none other than Paris Hilton, in a city I'd only dreamed about as a child, clad in gorgeous designer clothes and accessories, and still feeling the glow from the love of so many wonderful friends who had celebrated a beautiful New Year's Eve with us. I fully recognized I quite literally had it all. It was the life I'd so desperately desired for so many years. My subscriptions to *Us Weekly* and *People Magazine* had been the basis for a kind of constant, rotating vision board for my wildest dreams, and it had manifested beyond anything I could have expected. I was standing in the kitchen of Paris Hilton's old home, for Christ's sake!

And yet ... I knew this was not my right life. I was meant for more. More meaning. More connection with the man I was married to. More fulfillment for the deeper parts of me that did not come to this planet solely for an Instagram-perfect life. But as was the case in so many wee hours of so many mornings, I pushed that niggling little voice down to the recesses of my being. I told myself these were trivial problems.

Who cared if my marriage was unhappy? I had friends to fill in the gaps in intimacy. Who cared if I suspected I was poisoning my body with a steady stream of alcohol, drugs, and facial injectables while starving it of nourishment? At least I could finally look in the mirror without feeling disgust. Who cared about my sneaking suspicion that there was work I was meant to be doing that would actually help people? I had an American Express Centurion black card with unlimited spending. The holes in my soul could surely be filled with one more perfect outfit, one more girls' trip to London, or one more bottle of bubbly.

So I looked in the ornate foyer mirror and reminded myself how blessed I was. Then I climbed the stairs, washed my face, and fell into the cushy guest room bed. I was too tired to deal with my husband and our earlier conflict. He'd been asleep in the master bedroom for several hours and likely would not wake up if I slipped into bed. But as was the case on so many occasions, the thought of sharing energy with him in such close proximity was simply too much to bear in my exhausted, depleted, and soon-to-be hung-over state. Hopefully, we could gloss over this fight in the morning, and I'd be out the door and on my way to sharing an Ivy Gimlet (or four) with our visiting friends for New Year's Day brunch. If I could spread out my party binge long enough, maybe he would forget about this particular incident, and we could just move on. And so the well-seeded pattern of conflict and creeping separateness in our marriage continued to grow.

The Beginning

I met my husband on New Year's Eve, 2001. I'd just moved into a small but stylish loft in a historic old hotel in downtown Houston that had been converted into apartments. I'd gone to the gym in the basement, and while on the treadmill, a cute guy got on the broken exercise bike next to me and introduced himself. It turned out he was interested in more than working out.

He invited me to a New Year's party at his loft upstairs that evening. Although I'd planned to celebrate solo with a *Sex and the City* marathon, I acquiesced and showed up to his party, which was filled with couples. So I introduced myself to the only other single gal I saw there. I would later learn that she and my future husband were quasi-involved. The night kinda went downhill from there.

When we reconnected several months later and finally went on our first date, it didn't end much better than New Year's had. There was a connection, though, and somehow things kept moving forward. Before I knew it, we were several months into a relationship. I applied to law school and was accepted at the University of Texas. He and his law partner, both UT alums, opened a second office of their firm in Austin, and collectively we all made our way to central Texas.

Our relationship was rife with conflict from the get. But he challenged and impressed me. We talked and debated politics, spirituality, philosophy, and social justice endlessly. Our values aligned well. He thought I was entertaining and funny, which fed my only-child craving for constant attention and validation. I was in awe of his business acumen, his courage, and the fact that he'd come from nothing to create a hugely successful law practice. We traveled the world together and partied with the best of them. And while his temper ran hot, underneath he was a kind man for whom family was of utmost importance.

I also knew he would be a stable provider and protector – although I wince in embarrassment and shame as I write these words. How does one convey a soul connection while also acknowledging the reality of the factors often under consideration when deciding who to marry? Many of the factors I assumed I needed to consider came directly from the entrenched Southern traditions that still exist in old-fashioned hometowns like mine.

For me, it began in Tyler, a city in far East Texas where my grandparents settled during the oil boom of the 1930s. The town was fairly small and was no cultural epicenter – I remember the buzz of excitement in the community when we got our first Olive Garden restaurant in the mid-90s. Tyler did, however, become home to some very deep pockets of old oil money, of which it was very proud. The self-proclaimed Rose Capital of the World, it boasted a historic country club and golf course, the Azalea Trail, and a debutante festival meant to rival those of the East Coast.

In this cultural soup that I found myself in, the messaging was very clear: Women don't create wealth; they marry men who do. The more wealth your man creates, the better. Gold stars to the women who didn't have to work. I also don't remember seeing a lot of love among the couples I was beginning to observe for clues as to what made up a successful marriage. From what I gathered, it was more important to put forth a perfect life than to have the substance to back it up behind closed doors. There really were no female entrepreneurs among the mothers in my friend group, save for a few family-owned businesses where the wife contributed her time. Other woman-owned businesses were usually pet projects funded by husbands and not moneymakers in their own right.

It was from these ingredients that I fashioned my marriage story. It was a belief system about what a marriage should look and feel like, from its external appearance to its intimate inner workings. I carried this marriage story with me as I made my way into adulthood with my list of acceptable criteria for a potential spouse and our life together. My future husband fit the bill plus some. So after several years of dating, when he proposed at sunset on a beach in Santa Barbara to a backdrop of dolphins playing in the surf, I accepted with excitement.

A wedding for the ages followed. Looking back on it now, the sheer extravagance feels both selfish and shocking ... but oh, it was beautiful. There was a ceremony on the rolling lawn of the Four Seasons Hotel in Austin, complete with a full gospel choir, Sylvia Weinstock cake, fireworks over Lady Bird Lake, and a vintage Rolls Royce to carry us away to our future. It was pretty magical. And then came marriage, a jarring reality where our already high level of conflict seemed only to increase.

Fight Club: The Marriage Edition

From the very beginning, our relationship was extremely combative. We were two strong-willed attorneys whose personalities meshed like kerosene and fire. Our fights were explosive and frequent. I remember the overpowering embarrassment I felt after some of the more intense knock-down-drag-outs. I was always afraid to make eye contact with our neighbors or the concierge at our building for fear that they might have heard the screams and slamming doors. I remember meals out – eaten while attempting to hold back tears, the waiter tentatively approaching, unsure of how to handle the awkward situation. I remember birthdays, anniversaries, parties, and big events marred by conflict.

Despite a lot of counseling, we still experienced a lot of anger, resentment, and, often, a mutual desire to strangle one another. Repeatedly, we'd pledge to "become ducks" – our code for letting the little stuff roll off our backs – but time and time again, we were unsuccessful. We were no model spouses. We were, however, both stubborn and committed, so we stuck with it until our heads were bloodied from beating them against that unyielding wall that was our marriage.

As my husband's wealth grew, so did my tolerance for conflict, at least for a while. It was easy to emotionally check out and hide from the glaring deficiencies in our relationship when we rarely saw each other from opposite ends of our 8,000-square-foot Austin penthouse – we got along much better when we didn't share a room – or even better, from opposite ends of the country, as I found myself in L.A. with increasing regularity.

But forces were coalescing in the shadows that would eventually come to a head. I attended Burning Man for the first time (more to come about this annual experimental living and art festival in Chapter 4), and realized the social skin I'd been wearing might not actually reflect who I really was. Was it possible that at heart I was happiest as a crunchy, nature-loving, nudie hippie?

I also found the writing of Dr. Martha Beck – or rather, it found me – while waiting at a dentist's office and held captive to their *O Magazine* reading material. Although I was not familiar with her at the time, Martha was soon to become one of the teachers of my heart. With three degrees from Harvard, including a PhD, she later became a *New York Times* bestselling author and, according to USA Today, the best-known life coach in America. That day at the dentist's office, I had stumbled upon one of her regular columns for O. In it, Martha wrote about Fang and Buddy – the names she gave for our "social" and "essential" selves. A light bulb went off: It became clear that virtually my entire life had been lived for others (i.e., for the social self), and my essential self was withering on the vine.

Soon, the disconnect between my external and internal life could not be ignored. It felt like a wedge in my very being, and it was tearing me apart. I'd arrived at the pinnacle of my seemingly perfect life ... and I knew I needed to leave it all. It made no rational sense, but it felt like a life-and-death decision – I somehow knew I would die if I continued on my current path. And even if physical death didn't find me in short order, I had a strong hunch that my essential self, the wisest part of me that was connected to something greater, might just give up on me. I felt that this part was eternal, but it simply might not stick around if I continued to live a life that was so out of my integrity and not at all reflective of my real truth – a truth I was only beginning to discover. It was a prospect I could no longer stomach. And frankly, I was done carrying the cumulative pain in my marriage borne from years of fighting, despite valiant efforts by both parties to find peace in our home.

One evening, I was catching up on the phone with Brooke, a dear college roommate who'd seen me through the wildest parts of my transition from teen years into adulthood, and who'd stood as a bridesmaid when I ultimately got married. I loved this gal for many reasons, not the least of which was that she had always accepted me fully and never passed judgment, no matter how crazy the story. She was actually the first married friend who revealed to me that her relationship was not all sunshine and roses. This was unheard of in my book – no matter the level of dysfunction or even abuse, you didn't talk about it. Just smile and worry more about what everyone else is thinking than the hard lump in your chest – you can cry on the bathroom floor later when no one else is around. So it was that on this evening, with this most understanding of friends, that I found myself saying before I could stop the words, "Brooke, I'm going to leave my marriage." There was a moment of silence as Brooke thoughtfully took in my words and crafted a nonplussed response so typical of her. No questions, no requests for gory details. Just: "Okay, my dear. Lemme know how I can support you."

Self-Imposed Chaos

We create chaos when we avoid the truth.
NANCY LEVIN

I'd known for a while that I needed out of my marriage, but in the most avoidant and juvenile of ways, I started acting out instead. Bestselling author and Hay House Radio personality Nancy Levin describes this so eloquently, pointing out that, "We create chaos when we avoid the truth." During Nancy's own marriage, she left a journal lying around the home she shared with her husband. In it, she had written about an affair she'd had several years prior. She calls that act of unconsciously (but not so subtly) leaving in plain view a journal containing divorce-worthy personal details "the bomb" she set for herself. She'd known for a long time her marriage had run its course, but she acknowledged it was easier to let her husband take the tough action of actually bringing things to an end upon learning of her affair. I, too, had some major truth about my marriage that I'd been dodging.

Although I don't think I was ready or brave enough to acknowledge it in my conscious awareness, I began pushing the limits of what any marriage can take, in cowardly hopes that my husband would do the dirty work and throw me out. That way, I wouldn't have to say the most difficult words in the world: I cannot go on like this, and I want out.

I almost got my wish soon thereafter when I stumbled in the door wasted at 7 a.m. after a hard night of partying with my best girlfriend. My husband was in a rage, and rightfully so – this type of behavior had been escalating for months. He stormed around my bedroom, collecting my credit cards and threatening to cut me off completely. Once my biggest fear ever, I just didn't care anymore. In fact, I felt relief that it might finally be over. Even in my drunken state, however, I will never forget the tears in his eyes as he stormed out of my room, kicking a pile of clothes near the door and saying with the most intense visceral emotion in his voice, "Why don't you care more about us?" I didn't have an answer for him at the moment. Stuffing what little guilt and shame could be felt through my alcohol-induced haze, I passed out.

When it was all said and done, I was the one to pull the plug. Although there were many deposits and withdrawals from our love account over the course of our twelve years together, we sadly hit a point where we'd been overdrawn for too long. There simply was nothing left to draw from. And really, I am not so sure how solid our foundation was to begin with – after spending a lifetime more worried about what other people thought than anything else, I'd created a life that was not reflective of who

I really was. My husband, on the other hand, was a different story.

Eleven years my senior when we met, he was oh-so-comfortable in his own skin; he was sure of what he wanted, and he knew what a mature, long-term commitment looked like. I, on the other hand, was an entitled and bratty 23-year old who could barely see past a fairytale wedding (which we had) to the business of an actual marriage. My husband was unfortunately first a witness to, then a victim of, my thrashing about from my early 20s into mid-life as my beliefs and I grew and changed – about love and life and God. All the while, I simultaneously wanted to be taken care of but quickly became resentful when I felt disempowered by the stark reality of who really held the purse strings in our home. Immaturity and "poor, poor, pitiful me" pouting at its finest.

I finally began to take some serious personal inventory in my mid-30s. As I shed the layers of my social self, revealing for the first time the essential self I'd ignored for so long, I realized that what I truly wanted in a lifelong partnership was much different than what my marriage offered. This discrepancy was made all the more obvious due to the mortal combat happening on a regular basis in our house.

In the end, I had to acknowledge my marriage just was not working for me. Sadly, my husband would bear the brunt of my change of heart. While I felt an ardent appreciation for him and an abiding gratitude for the life we'd created, I knew I had to leave. He deserved better than a wife who no longer wanted to be there. He deserved someone who was head-over-heels in love with him. He deserved someone who could look at him without anger, resentment, and contempt. Really, we both deserved more.

I fully recognize there are people out there who would have stuck things out. They would have stayed because they made a commitment and they entered into vows in front of family, friends, and the God of their understanding. For better or worse, I was no longer one of those people. I was no longer willing to sacrifice my own happiness and fulfillment to satisfy the expectations of others, of my culture, or of questionable religious dogma. And certainly not in service of an institution, the sanctity of which I was beginning to question.

I don't think my husband was surprised when I proposed that we separate. I found a small studio apartment in Austin, and with my dog and cat in tow, I packed up a few belongings and left.

Have Ring and Car, Will Travel

Our three-month separation turned into six months. During that time we'd meet for counseling once a week. These sessions were intended to give voice to our shared narrative so we could put that past behind us, regardless of whether we ultimately decided to reconcile or dissolve our union. We'd agreed that if either of us reached a point where we believed reconciliation was impossible, we would let the other know, out of respect. I hit that point in March 2012. I think if I'd been braver, I would have acknowledged hitting this point even sooner. But after a couple years of behavior I was none too proud of, I wanted to make my best effort before calling it, and I just couldn't seem to muster the courage to speak that truth any earlier. So it was that during a couple's therapy session on a cool spring morning, I said the hardest words I've ever had to utter: "I'm sorry. I cannot get back together with you."

I had so many concerns about the future when I made that declaration. I feared nuclear warfare in our divorce proceedings – my husband was a master in a courtroom, and I knew he could work the system in his favor with his eyes closed. I feared making the worst mistake of my life, one that would be irreparable. I also feared what our division of assets would look like, as I'd put myself in a rather precarious situation on that front.

Before our marriage, my husband wanted a prenuptial agreement; I, on the other hand, had been offended by the very idea. I begrudgingly agreed to one, but did little to facilitate creation of what I viewed as a loathsome document. As a result, my husband, procrastinator that he was, presented me with a hefty stack of paper less than a month before the wedding with advice from counsel that this probably was not the best way to go about the process. We'd then agreed to postpone completion until after the wedding by doing a postnuptial agreement – the fights about the prenup were kinda killing the romance of the whole wedding situation.

But we never completed that postnup. Despite many sessions with a CPA-turned-therapist, we had a heckuva time settling on a formula for dividing the assets. In the meantime, as a show of good faith until we executed a postnup, I signed documents giving up my rights to any property we acquired along the way. Where normally a married couple in Texas would split their shared assets, all the property was in my husband's name, so there was little that was shared. Not even homes or bank accounts. To boot, there was no postnuptial agreement to allocate anything to me.

All along, I questioned what self-respecting attorney would put herself in such a stupid situation. In short, I was potentially screwed. In fact, there was a point when I believed I would likely walk away with just my wedding ring and my car. By then, however, I was fueled by my anger and an intense desire for freedom. I also trusted that the Universe had my back, and I would eventually land on my feet, no matter how the divorce and allocation of assets shook out.

Ultimately, a couple of expert CPAs cobbled together a few unexpected shared assets to come up with a surprisingly respectable community estate. My soon-to-be ex-husband softened a bit, and I received a chunk that, while nowhere near the size of the total estate, was enough to purchase a modest house and comfortably take care of me for the next several years. It quite literally bought me some time to regain my foothold on sanity and come back home to myself after years of spinning out of control.

Making Way for Better Things

In December 2011, during my separation, I returned to the L.A. house for what I suspected would be the final time. Having signed away my right to that house upon its purchase, it was never really mine to begin with. But I had loved it dearly and we'd made so many fun, beautiful memories there. This time, there was no party. The house felt still and calm. I said my goodbyes, promising to return someday on different terms.

The years that followed brought new love, an unanticipated awesome post-divorce friendship with my ex-husband, and meaningful work. Most importantly, I began to live from the place of my wisest, most essential self. I traded Instagram-perfect for authenticity and honesty. I chose empowerment over the cloak of protection offered by my old life and my husband's success. And while I still get scared or feel twinges of longing for that life from time to time, I know I am not supposed to go back. Although it doesn't always make sense, all I have to do is just envision stepping back into that life, and I immediately feel a hard lump in my chest, my signal that something is leading me away from my right life. Instead, I am now following the call of my heart and soul toward something more.

I left a great deal behind when I left my marriage, not the least of which was a man who, despite our conflict, loved me dearly in his own unique way. But sometimes things have to fall apart to make way for better things. While my journey is nowhere near complete, so many better things have already happened for me. And better things await you, too. It is my hope for you, dear reader, that this book will inspire and empower you to something more, whatever that looks like in your life.

CHAPTER 3

My Process: The Steps to Courage, Clarity, and a Better Life

*For the hero who refuses the call to adventure, all he can do
is create new problems for himself and await the gradual
approach of his disintegration.*
JOSEPH CAMPBELL, *The Hero with a Thousand Faces*

It was around the time when my marital dysfunction and chaos was at a feverish pitch that my cosmic alarm clock went off, and I had a deep knowing that I would soon need to implode my life spectacularly. Amidst the confusion and fear I experienced as I worried about when I would need to act and how everything could possibly work out for the best, I adopted a little internal mantra that I repeated with increasing frequency as things began to escalate: "Peace. Peace. Peace. Peace..."

I'd desired peace for such a long time. My marriage had been many things, but peaceful was not one of them. For years, I'd tried to liken our constant bickering to the endearing back-and-forth nattering of an old married couple. This comparison just wasn't true, however. Our conflict was exhausting, and I needed a break. There wasn't much, in fact, that was peaceful about the rest of my life, either. Constantly on the run from the truth and with a steady stream of booze and stimulants in my system, I buzzed from one party and trip to the next. My mind, body, and spirit were addled and exhausted, too. I needed peace in my life, and I needed peace and clarity about my decision to leave.

I'm not quite sure where I originally got the idea (probably *O Magazine*, my gateway drug to all things self-help and spiritual), but I also became a bit obsessed with getting congruent between my head, heart, and gut. For so many years, my mind and mind alone had guided most of my decisions. It was mind that was concerned with what others thought; it was mind that worried I'd end up alone and broke if I were to leave my marriage; it was mind that tried to convince me that a simple list of pros and cons would suffice in deciding how to proceed in my marriage.

There's an old proverb that says, "The mind is a wonderful servant but a terrible master." (Correct attribution of this quote is a bit dodgy.) My mind had been my master for many years. While I had to thank my mind for doing a bang-up job at the rational, logical tasks it made possible (Law school, anyone?), it hadn't always steered me right when functioning solo on more nuanced decisions about my right life.

So I knew that for a decision of this magnitude, I would need to include more than mind. Going forward, I enlisted the best my being had to offer, consulting with head (the seat of analytic thinking in the brain), heart (the seat of love and an organ that actually sends more information to the brain than vice versa), and gut (the seat of intuition and inner wisdom) on all matters. Relying on this powerful trifecta, I set about the business of facing and making some tough decisions about my marriage.

Although for many years, mind had feigned confusion about the right course of action, once heart and gut got involved, I had to admit I wasn't confused. In fact, I knew what I needed to do. I'd just been too scared – mind had thrown up too many roadblocks, too many doomsday scenarios, for me to listen to my truth. Ultimately, I got radically honest with myself, and then my husband, finally admitting that I needed to step away from our life.

More than anything else, the peace mantra and bringing heart and gut into the game were survival mechanisms and comforting touchstones for me at the time. Although mantras and mind-body connections were previously unknown to me, it was almost as if my wise, essential self had mercifully gone on autopilot, and was locking in on a beacon to guide me home. I was slowly-but-surely getting the courage I needed to move forward and the clarity that I was making the right decision. It was from these practices that my coaching process was born.

My Process

In the years that followed, I threw myself into healing work. First for myself, then later for my coaching clients. From ayahuasca journeys to hypnotherapy to sound healing, I was willing to try just about anything to feel better, to confirm that I'd made the right decision, and to continue moving forward courageously, despite terror barriers that felt insurmountable. Over time, a process organically emerged. It tracked my own healing journey, except without all the stumbles I made along my way.

Through this process, I also created a new life, one that reflected the most real, essential me. For so many years, I'd remained stuck in fear of what that life would look like – I was unwilling to leave without some assurance that it was absolutely the right decision and that my life would be better on the other side. Once I made the leap, the life that rose up to catch me was exactly what my heart and spirit had desired and envisioned. That's not to say it's been free of challenges and hard work. It has, however, absolutely been worth it. And this book you are reading is but one bit of proof of what is possible when you "give up the life you planned in order to embrace the life that is waiting for you." (Hat tip to Joseph Campbell.)

Over the course of the next few chapters, I will share my process with you. It's the best of the resources and tools I've curated. These steps worked for me, and they work for my clients. And now, they can work for you, too. Although you can approach this book however your head, heart, and gut lead you, these steps are typically best done in order. They build upon each other, with the more advanced maneuvers toward the end, after you have developed a strong foundation from which to work.

What to Expect

Step One will get you in touch with the wisest, most essential part of yourself. It's the most authentic part of your being, the part that knows the plan for your best life and always has your highest interest in mind. Some call this your higher self; others call it the essential self. For purposes of this book, we'll call it your Wise Authentic Self.

Although most adults have not been given the tools for accessing this part of themselves, it's always there. But it often speaks softly, much softer than the cacophony of chatter from our inner critic, our fear, or even the external voices of friends, family, and others. The key is to get connected to your Wise Authentic Self, first and foremost. From that vantage point, you have access to the best guidance and intuition available that is uniquely suited to you and your life.

But just because you've found your authentic self and know how to access its wisdom, doesn't mean the rest is just smooth sailing. Fear and limiting beliefs may still pop up, causing confusion and self-doubt. What's more, you've likely had decades to develop a belief system about love, marriage, and divorce. What you have been told or absorbed about these things may contradict what your Wise Authentic Self begins to whisper to you about your own truth. Step Two is all about dissolving the painful and limiting beliefs that keep you stuck, and confidently owning what is true for you.

At some point along the way, you will likely get angry or sad or experience profound grief. In Step Three, I'll show you how to feel all the feels, even the uncomfortable ones, in a gentle, safe way. Allowing for our emotions is not, as I used to think, like opening Pandora's Box. Your body knows just what to do with all of your feelings, and it is designed to embrace them all. This step will show you how.

Then we're on to Step Four: self-love. I myself resisted this step mightily for many years, but in my experience, it's a must. In fact, it might just be the most significant component in all of our work together. Like me, you may think it sounds fluffy, meaningless, and even selfish. I assure you, it is not! Humor me, if you will, and you may just find it feels pretty good to take care of that Wise Authentic Self of yours. When you do, you will likely find that your connection to your inner wisdom and intuition is much stronger and that you have a greater sense of happiness and overall well-being.

Step Five is all about creating a vision for your future. When your current situation seems bleak or the going gets tough (as can happen when making tough decisions about your marriage or navigating divorce), you will have something to look forward to. Your dreams and schemes for your future will serve as a light at the end of the tunnel – a light you create!

It's so much easier to make difficult decisions when they don't feel life and death and you don't feel so alone. In Step Six, you will gain valuable perspective that will allow you to breathe easier as you make your way forward and take action. Spoiler alert: this perspective comes by way of spirituality. But this ain't no religion and there is no dogma – promise! This is actually where you'll really solidify your connection to that head, heart, and gut trifecta.

Now is the time where you'll really get to test your mettle and see how honest you can get with an inventory of self. Step Seven will take you on a journey of compassion and radical honesty, which will be rewarded with a sense of radical empowerment. Instead of a victim, you'll be more like Wonder Woman, ready to take on whatever your marriage or your life throws at you!

Like the archetypal hero in Joseph Campbell's *The Hero With a Thousand Faces*, you, too, will likely face some challenges along the way. Answering the call to get unstuck in a bad marriage is a hero's journey, and obstacles are inherent in such a journey. But overcoming those obstacles is what makes you a champion when you come out the other side. In Step Eight, I'll share some of the most common challenges you may encounter, as well as tools for dealing with them.

Finally, Step Nine. By this point in our work together, you may find that divorce is in the highest and best interest of all involved. If so, rest assured that divorce does not always have to be devastating. You can mitigate emotional, relational, and spiritual damages to yourself and others by approaching the process gracefully. In this final step, I will provide gentler legal options, as well as tips and suggestions for creating the best possible outcomes, should you decide to leave your marriage.

Ready, Set, Go Toward Your Best Life

Many unhappy couples stay married for a lifetime simply because they are too fearful of leaving an unsatisfying but tolerable life together. And having witnessed some nuclear warfare divorces among friends or in the media that left the parties dried up, angry shells of people, you may be scared into staying in a bad relationship indefinitely.

That, however, is why I'm so passionate about the work that I now do and the process I've outlined in this book. You didn't come here to live a passable existence in a crappy relationship. You came here for more, and you deserve more. With the process outlined in this book, you absolutely can have the courage and the clarity to make the right decision about your marriage, as well as have an awesome new life on the other side of divorce. I am living proof. And while our legal system around divorce has the potential to leave some gaping wounds, my process will leave you whole. Perhaps more whole than when you began this journey.

Along the way you may get scared and feel some resistance. That's okay – I did too. In such cases, I invite you to use your resistance as a compass. As author Steven Pressfield so eloquently puts it, "The more important a call or action is to our soul's evolution, the more resistance we will feel toward pursuing it." But your resistance will "unfailingly point to true north" and guide you "to that calling or action that we must follow over all others."

This process also calls for focus and a strong connection to your wisest, best self. Racehorses wear blinders so they can stay set on the finish line without getting spooked or distracted by what's going on around them. In much the same way, I encourage you to adopt a similar practice. Create your own metaphoric racehorse blinders that can keep you from worrying about what's behind you or what could take you off-course. This is your race, and the prizes are clarity, courage, and a fulfilling new life.

By the end of this book, you will have the tools to recognize and follow the actions you must take, as well as a connection to a wellspring of courage that will fuel your journey. Now, like those focused racehorses, put on your blinders and get ready to run toward your best life!

CHAPTER 4

Your Wise Authentic Self

From an early age, we are conditioned to ignore the voice within when considering who we are and what our goals are, and instead to look outward – to our family, friends, church, community, and even our critics ... If you refuse to listen to anybody long enough, she'll stop speaking. Which is why one day, we selfless women realize we can't hear our own voice.
GLENNON DOYLE MELTON

Part I – Your Small Self

The Friend Who Used To Run My Life

I want to introduce you to a friend of mine. Her name is Ms. Holly Wood. I've known her since birth, although we haven't always been close. She has a killer wardrobe that hangs perfectly on her tiny, borderline-unhealthy frame. She is well-educated. She has a beautiful home in the hills of L.A. Yet despite all the trappings of a perfect life, she lives in a constant state of fear. Fear of not being enough ... not smart enough, not pretty enough, not thin enough, not wealthy enough... the list goes on and on.

Who is this Holly person? She's actually a facet of me. Holly is the part that developed in response to the people around me, like my parents, friends, teachers, religious leaders, and my Southern culture. She's the "social self" mentioned in Chapter 2. She's the part of me that lives eternally in comparison mode, constantly asking whether I am better than or less than those around me. And she desperately needs to identify with external things, like the work I do, my social status, education, physical appearance, special abilities, relationships, personal and family history, belief systems, and even political, nationalistic, and racial identifications.

I've come to call this part of me my Small Self. Because so much of my life and self-worth had been wrapped up in my connection to Los Angeles, it just made sense to call her first name: Holly, last name: Wood. While Ms. Holly Wood's name is definitely pun intended, it very seriously encompasses everything my Small Self glommed onto from an early age.

Fitting In at Any Cost

Whether you call it the social self (as Martha does), the Small Self (as I and so many others do), or something else entirely, it really matters not. The key thing to remember is this aspect of our psyche wants us to fit in. In fact, as humans we are hardwired from birth with an intense drive to be socially compatible with others. It's a survival thing.

Millennia ago, fitting in and remaining with the tribe was necessary to stay alive in a harsh and unsafe world. Although tribe membership is no longer mandatory for our physical survival, the urge to fit in remains ingrained. The problem is that our Small Self may not always have our best interest at heart. In its effort to keep us safe by ensuring we are acting appropriately and thereby accepted by others, it may well steer us away from the truest desires of our heart.

So we find ourselves as little girls taking dance instead of piano, because that is what the cool kids do; we end up becoming a doctor instead of an artist, simply because that is what our father hoped for or expected of us; or we end up joining Garden Club instead of that pole dancing class that secretly sounded really fun, because what would the women in our church group think?

Up until several years ago, when I finally realized Holly was merely an *aspect* of me, not the whole me, she ran my life with an iron fist. Every decision I made was in service of Holly and her insatiable desires and fears. But it was never enough for Holly. With each pound lost, with each degree earned, with each dollar added to the already sizeable bank account, she still compared and despaired. She made a lot of hollow promises that when she got the next thing, whatever it was, she would leave me alone. But that never happened, because our Small Selves, like the hungry ghosts described in Chinese Buddhism, are never satisfied.

The good news is that your Small Self is not the whole of your psyche. You've got other parts knocking around in there, the most important being your Wise Authentic Self. It's the real you, the part that transcends space and time and physical circumstances. It encompasses your strengths and weaknesses, your preferences, abilities, and what makes you laugh. It's the part that would remain constant and unchanged whether you were raised in North America, Asia, or Africa, or whether your family was Christian, Hindu, or Muslim.

While your Small Self is distracted by the shiny objects of this world, your Wise Authentic Self is more interested in the light that makes them shine. Where your Small Self feels anxious and separate, your Wise Authentic Self securely recognizes its connection to others, to the outside world, and the larger tapestry of life. Your Wise Authentic Self is the seat of your soul, if you believe you have one of those. And while your Small Self is often myopically and fearfully focused on achieving more, doing more, and accumulating more stuff, your Wise Authentic Self contains the passionate callings of your heart and houses the bigger vision of who you *really* are and your true life purpose.

Complicating matters, the leanings of your Wise Authentic Self often exist in direct opposition to the graspings of your Small Self. For example, while your Wise Authentic Self may desire you to leave your soul-sucking corporate job for a career in the healing arts, your Small Self will likely be the first to pipe up and tell you that such a switch is impractical and reckless – and besides, what are your friends, family, and current colleagues going to say? Or your Wise Authentic Self may whisper that you are in the wrong marriage, while your Small Self may scream that to leave would mean public embarrassment, shame, and irrevocable loss.

If this sounds familiar, I feel your pain. Just a few short years ago, I found myself in this very same conundrum of Small Self versus Wise Authentic Self. After years of caving to Small Self concerns, however, this time I chose the path of my Wise Authentic Self.

My Small Self Goes Up in Flames

We arrived at the gates of Burning Man in August 2010. It was my first time at this crazy desert festival. It was a surprise trip for my then-husband after he'd complained incessantly that we just didn't have enough fun in our lives. Selfishly, I'd wanted to check off this bucket list item for years, so this seemed like a good place to kill two birds with one fire: I could go wild in the desert, and my husband would finally have no excuse for not having fun in this over-the-top festival of art, sound, dust, and love that puts Vegas to shame.

As is customary for virgin Burners, I rang the large metal entry gate bell as we crossed the threshold into Black Rock City, the temporary town populated by 70,000 festival-goers for the duration of the ten-day event. What I would never be able to un-ring from that moment forward was the feeling of shedding my social skin for the first time in my life. Although I did not have a vocabulary full of coach-y terms like Small Self and Wise Authentic Self at the time, something felt decidedly different on the playa of this ancient seabed in a remote corner of Nevada.

As attendees traded their street clothes for steam punk garb, loincloths, or just plain shirt-cocking nudity, I noticed something else. The social distinctions were falling away, as well. There was no way to tell whether the person next to you on the ornate art car was a CEO for a Fortune 500 company or a lifelong intentional nomad, both of whom had come from around the world to share in the utopian goodness this crazy city of Black Rock had to offer.

People from all walks of life were present with no pressure to look a certain way or be anything other than what simply felt good. I exhaled a huge sigh of relief and followed it with an inhale big enough to draw in this magical place where I didn't have to be a perfect wife, a respectable attorney, or certain rung on the social ladder. I could just be me.

And then in quick succession, an equally large realization followed: Because I'd created an entire life around my Small Self, I wasn't really sure who I was underneath it all. But I was now committed to finding out.

Coming Home to Self

When we left Burning Man that first year and returned to Austin after several weeks in an RV, the palatial penthouse where we lived no longer felt like home. The 8,000 square feet of luxury upon which much of my identity rested, and in which I'd so proudly lived and entertained, suddenly felt embarrassingly excessive. I didn't need all this space. The 20-foot ceilings were too tall. We had too much stuff. It was all just too much.

I had lived in relative simplicity in the motor coach we'd inhabited during our Burning Man road trip adventure. Turns out the RV life at which I'd turned up my nose for so many years was something my Wise Authentic Self really loved. Who knew? I did now, and there was no turning back.

I began to question what other things I'd surrounded myself with did not actually reflect who I really was. For the first time, I began to articulate my own values – not my parents', friends' or culture's values, but *mine.* This exploration snowballed, and where I'd once believed that more would never be enough to make me feel complete, I realized this was far from reality. My heart had been cracked wide open by experiencing the generosity and radical acceptance practiced at Burning Man. I wanted more of that!

I also knew that whatever decision I made around my unhappy marriage needed to come from the wisest, most authentic part of me. And although this part of me had an intense love and appreciation for my then-husband, I soon realized that it had been my Small Self (a.k.a. Ms. Holly Wood) that had been in the front seat of our relationship, from dating to wedding to marriage. It was as if I was living in an arranged marriage orchestrated by Holly based on her most esteemed values (i.e., external perfection). But I now knew from personal experience that true happiness can only come from the Wise Authentic Self who bucks social expectations and keeping up appearances in favor of what feeds the heart and soul.

Who's the Friend Running Your Life?

Now it is your turn, dear reader, to get in touch with your Small Self – and you don't have to attend Burning Man to figure it out (unless you want to, of course)! The following exercise will help you identify the friend, the Small Self part of your psyche, who may be running your life and pressuring you to look, be, and act in a certain way. This part likely has very specific opinions about your spouse and your marriage.

For this and the exercises in the chapters to follow, I invite you to get out a journal and a pen and keep them handy. Using the prompts below, we are going to tap into your Small Self, describing this part of you down to the most minute detail. When you're ready, use the following questions to create a picture in your journal of your Small Self:

What does your Small Self look like? Describe its frame and any physical characteristics. Does it look human, or does it have the likeness of some other creature or mythical being? What is it wearing? Does it have any accessories with it?

Do you get a sense of where it lives? For Holly, it is poolside in a cabana at my former L.A. home. But maybe your Small Self is most at home in that corner partner's office ... or smugly sitting in lotus position at an impressive silent meditation retreat ... or at the podium as head of the PTA at your kids' school. Just notice where it is most at home, where it most wants to be.

If the Small Self's job is to constantly compare whether you are better than or worse than others, what are the subjects it is most obsessed with? For me and Holly, remember, it was how thin, how educated, and how wealthy I was compared to my peers and the celebrities I followed. So what is your Small Self's obsession? Physical fitness? A certain accomplishment or credential? Living in a particular neighborhood in your city? Your kids' scholastic or athletic performance? Or even how spiritual or religious you are?

And what other things does your Small Self glom onto? Your family history or status, a certain political party, or collective identification, like your country of residence?

Also, what does your Small Self have to say about your marriage? Holly consistently reminded me that my internal happiness and marital satisfaction were far less important than the external image I put forth. Her advice? Stay put, despite the intense misgivings of my heart and spirit. What is your Small Self encouraging you to do or not do in your relationship?

Finally, now that you have a picture of what your Small Self looks like, what will you name it? Or perhaps it has very clearly demanded it be called something in particular. The practice of naming this part of yourself is actually rooted in neuroscience. You are placing yourself in the observer position. In other words, this is a recognition that you are not your Small Self. You are something larger that does not have to cater to or live by the whims of the Small Self.

So, meet your Small Self. Picture it in your mind's eye. And as hard as it may be, I invite you to thank it for doing its best to keep you safe. Remember, it really just wants you to be accepted so you survive.

And now, send it back to its home, just as I send Holly back to her poolside cabana with a glass of champagne to keep her busy for a while. For the work we are about to do around your marriage and how to proceed, you are going to want your Wise Authentic Self in the driver's seat!

Part II – Your Wise Authentic Self

Get Still

Now that you know how to recognize your Small Self and its wants and fears, it's time to get in touch with your Wise Authentic Self. Unlike the loud, alarmist voice of your Small Self, your Wise Authentic Self emanates peace. It communicates from the place of our most profound intuition. You can trust its guidance, and it will never tell you to harm yourself or another.

Because it speaks softly, however, you may need to practice a little stillness to hear it. Getting still doesn't mean you must become a mindfulness guru or an expert meditator. I certainly wasn't when I started this practice, mostly out of necessity to find some calm amidst all the chatter around me.

Try starting with this exercise: Sit comfortably in a quiet place. Place one hand over your heart to guide your awareness from your head to the heart space. Take several deep breaths, preferably through the nose (nose breathing triggers your parasympathetic nervous system to come online, which tells your body it's time to rest and digest). In this state of gentle relaxation and with your hand still over your heart, pose a question, such as "What do I need to know about my relationship?" See what comes back, and record it in your journal.

You may hear a word or phrase, you may see a color or an image, or you may receive nothing at all. Either way is fine. By simply showing up to listen on a consistent basis, even for just a few minutes a day, you will begin to strengthen your relationship with your intuition, values, and the voice of your Wise Authentic Self. With this practice in place, when the going gets tough or you find yourself in a pinch, your knee-jerk response will be to turn inward toward the guidance of your Wise Authentic Self while tuning out all the confusing and conflicting external noise.

Follow the Freedom

Move toward that which makes you feel most alive. In Japan, they call it waku waku. You can actually feel it in your body. It's your most reliable GPS for discovering your already-installed creative capital.
PAM GROUT, *Thank & Grow Rich*

"I just don't know what to do," Marcy said as she slumped forward exhaustedly, putting her head in her hands. "My family doesn't believe in divorce and my friends don't understand how I can even consider leaving such a comfortable life – they all just keep telling me that marriage is hard work and I need to stick it out." I looked up from the notes I was taking and asked her, "Well, what do *you* want to do?" Marcy responded in exasperation, "That's just it – I don't know what I want to do. On paper, my life looks great ... but I'm just so unhappy in my marriage. How am I supposed to know what to do, and what if I make the wrong choice?"

It is sessions and questions like these that take me back to my own indecision around whether to stay or go. Like Marcy, I'd weighed the pros and cons and thought through every possible outcome ad nauseam. I was inundated with information and opinions from others, and my mind just spun and spun in the same familiar loops. Meanwhile, I remained stuck as my inability to make a decision incapacitated me. I knew there had to be something I was missing, some source of vital input that I could turn to in this time of need.

Quite serendipitously, I found the answer when I discovered Martha Beck on that fateful day at the dentist. After reading her column in *O Magazine*, I was hooked. I promptly purchased every book she'd published and devoured them all in short order. I clung desperately to the wisdom in so much of her writing, but there was one particular excerpt that was more pivotal, more of a catalyst, than any other. I read and reread this dog-eared page over and over while I was working up the courage to make my move. This passage became an especially significant touchstone for me once I'd decided to leave – if I ever waivered in my conviction, I simply returned to it and would immediately feel the voice of my Wise Authentic Self gently pulling me up and away from my old life.

My go-to quote, paraphrased from the Buddha, went something like this: *When you encounter a body of water, you will know it is the ocean because it tastes of salt. In much the same way, you will know enlightenment and truth because it tastes of freedom ... not safety, not comfort, but freedom.* At the time, I had beaucoup de safety in my life. And comfort, well, my life was beyond comfortable. But freedom? Not so much.

My Small Self (a.k.a. Holly) didn't care so much about freedom. She liked safety and comfort. But that is what your Small Self does – it craves safety and predictability. It wants the known, even if the known is not healthy, because it is comfortable. I didn't want to listen to Holly anymore however, so I asked my Wise Authentic Self to take the lead. And that Self led me to the freedom I so desperately craved.

A quick aside: Freedom doesn't have anything to do with whether you are single, married, or anywhere in between. You could be partnered up for 50 years and feel that internal sense of freedom, or you could be single but shackled up to high heaven in other areas of your life. Bottom line, this is about whether your life allows for and supports the growth of your innermost, authentic self.

Now, perhaps you're wondering how in the world you're supposed to recognize freedom and follow it. Spoiler alert: Your body holds all the answers! Keeping your journal nearby, try the following exercise to see what I mean.

For the next few moments, recall an unpleasant memory. You might envision being back in that dead-end job that you hated with a boss who micromanaged your every move, or that recent blowup with your spouse that left you feeling raw and misunderstood, or that time you had to wait in a crawling airport security line when you were running late for a flight. Notice the physical sensations in your body as you hold this negative memory, and jot them down in your journal.

Although these sensations will be distinctive for your body, there will likely be some common threads, like muscular contraction and/or heaviness somewhere in the body. For me, my chest and throat clench up. For you, there may be knots in your stomach or an overall sense of intense weightiness. There is no right or wrong answer here, but chances are the sensations will be a bit unpleasant.

Freedom, on the other hand, should feel lighter and more pleasant. See what I mean by recalling a more positive memory. You can envision being with your child or companion animal, or sitting in a lounge chair at your favorite beach with a fruity drink in hand, or falling in love for the first time. Notice any physical sensations that come up, and write them down. Again, what you experience will be unique to you, but chances are the feeling will be more expansive, relaxed, and lighter than before. That, my friend, is freedom.

Your Wise Authentic Self thrives on freedom. Heck, our country was founded on it: Life, *Liberty* (read: freedom), and the Pursuit of Happiness. And you can follow that feeling of freedom like a compass pointing due north toward your right life.

That's exactly what Marcy did. During our session, I asked Marcy to put her own fears and doubts, as well as the outside opinions she'd been carrying, into a metaphoric box and place it high on a shelf – she could have all of it back at the end of the hour. I invited her to close her eyes, take a deep breath, and envision being with her husband. From that place, I asked her to describe the physical sensations in her body.

Immediately, she experienced a clenching and stabbing sensation in her gut. It most definitely did not feel like freedom; instead, her gut felt tight and constricted. While Marcy did not have to *do* anything with this information at the moment, I suggested she begin to notice how often in her marriage she experienced a tight, painful gut. Her body was clearly talking to her, and it was up to her if and when she listened to its messages and what they might indicate about her relationship.

After several months of work together, Marcy ultimately decided to leave. She faced some challenges along the way, which is completely normal, even in the best of divorce scenarios. However, following the freedom was empowering and energizing for her. She felt emboldened to make the decision she'd been unable to before, knowing now she was living in accordance with the guidance of her Wise Authentic Self.

Your F*ck It Phase

My dear friend Tara has a rare blood disease. The life expectancy for those with this disease decreases exponentially beyond the age of 40. Tara is now 44. Tara also survived an abdominal aortic aneurism while undergoing surgery to treat her disease. This type of aneurism has an overall mortality rate of 90 percent. Yeah, she's a bit miraculous.

During her aneurism, Tara had a near-death experience (NDE). Like most NDE survivors, on the other side of the veil she received the messages that she is dearly, unconditionally loved, that she is always safe, and that she is never alone. She also returned with a healthy dose of what she calls her "f*ck it" mentality. Living on borrowed time following an abdominal aortic aneurism will do that to a person.

Tara's "f*ck it" phase led her to take stock of her life and make some brave decisions. She unapologetically began to practice audacious self-care. She said no to invitations and activities that didn't feel good. And she was unafraid to look at her relationships (including her marriage) dead-on and weed out anything that wasn't nourishing.

Fortunately for you, it is statistically improbable that you will have to go through the whole rare blood disease / aneurism / NDE thing. However, you can learn a lot about the desires of your Wise Authentic Self by adopting your own "f*ck it" mentality. By throwing caution and your Small Self to the wind, even if just in your mind for a few brief minutes, you may discover some unexpected truths. And although your Wise Authentic Self cares greatly about all aspects of your life and being, for the purposes of this book, we're going to focus on connecting to its input specifically about your marriage. To access its voice and take a raw look at your relationship, grab that journal and follow the prompts below to take an honest look at your marriage:

A F*ck It Look at Your Marriage

When it comes to my marriage, if I didn't care what people (e.g., family, friends, pastor or church congregation, neighbors, community) thought, I would_____.

When it comes to my marriage, if I were sure that my actions would not hurt others in any way, I would_____.

When it comes to my marriage, if I had the courage, I would _____.

When it comes to my marriage, if I had total clarity that it was the right choice, I would_____.

When it comes to my marriage, if I could be certain it would not affect my children negatively, I would_____.

When it comes to my marriage, if I knew I would be okay financially, I would _____.

If I could be certain my life would be as good or even better following divorce, I would do the following when it comes to my marriage: _____.

Look back at how you filled in the blanks in the above exercise. What themes or common threads run through your answers? Do you now have a better sense of how your Wise Authentic Self might act with your Small Self out of the way?

If your answers scare you or point you in a direction you are not quite ready to go, that is okay! This exercise is merely meant to help you gather information and get in touch with a deeper part of yourself. You do not have to take any action yet, unless you feel inspired to do so.

Conclusion

Over the course of this chapter, you've learned to distinguish between your Small Self and your Wise Authentic Self. You know how to spot the voice of your Small Self, as well as its grasping desires and fears. You also know how to access your Wise Authentic Self and how it speaks to you. Like any good friendship, you will need to nurture your relationship with your Wise Authentic Self. Appreciate its quirks, learn to hear nuances in its whispers, and let it know that you want to hear what it has to say. In time, you'll be completing each other's sentences and laughing about those early times, when you were tentative and unsure around one another. Growing this relationship will serve you well for a lifetime. In fact, it might just be the most important relationship you ever have.

CHAPTER 5

Your Marriage Story

You are getting closest to your truth when you feel the most fear.
PEMA CHODRON

"**P**lease tell me about your background," I asked Amy, a new client who was confused about whether or not she wanted to remain in her marriage. She was well-educated and had a successful career as a high level executive with a large corporation, but she was really struggling to make decisions in her personal life. "Well, I'm not religious, but my mom is Catholic and my dad is Baptist. They've been married for over 50 years. I have a big, loving family, none of whom are divorced. The thought of being the first in my family to get a divorce just makes me feel like such a disappointment. It's like I know what I want to do ... but then I think about all of them and what they will say. Some of them are very religious and opposed to divorce. I'm just too scared to rock the boat."

Amy's situation is not uncommon. In addition to her own thoughts and opinions about marriage and divorce, she was carrying the weight of her entire family's thoughts and opinions, as well. As is the case for so many adults, her own adult values were not always aligned with those of her family of origin. But so many of the beliefs she'd been taught growing up were very powerfully ingrained, making it difficult for Amy to separate those from the beliefs she'd come to adopt after growing up and living on her own.

We all have a "marriage story" we carry into adulthood. It's an amalgamation of what we caught from simply being around and observing others as a child, and also what we were explicitly taught by the adults in our life. It encompasses what you think marriage is, what it isn't, the respective roles of the individuals involved, and all the "shoulds" and "should nots" that dictate one's behavior within and outside of the institution.

During my work with Amy, we identified the marriage story she was raised to believe, as well as identified a new marriage story that better reflected who she was as an independent and empowered adult. This gave her the peace and confidence she needed to make the best decision *for her* around whether to stay or go. The goal is to make sure the marriage story we decide to keep is as close to our own truth as possible. And where our marriage story conflicts with the marriage stories of those closest to us, to feel secure in having reached the bedrock of our own integrity so we can confidently own our choices.

For many years, I carried a marriage story that did not reflect my deepest truth. As a result, I was not only dragging around a story that was not mine, but also the confusion and shame of not being able to make that old marriage story work. You, too, may be living a marriage story that is not truly your own. In this chapter, you will have an opportunity to examine your own marriage story and decide whether it fits. If not, I will give you tools to create a new story, one that aligns with the deepest truth of who you are, and one that will allow you to make the right choices for you and your family.

My Marriage Story

We absorb a set of beliefs before we are old enough to think for ourselves, and unless we question them, they become the default lenses through which we enter into every situation we encounter.
GENEEN ROTH, *Lost and Found*

When I was growing up, my mother used to listen to *The Dr. Laura Program* on a little AM station in Tyler, Texas (for those who may not be familiar with her, I'm referring to the controversial radio personality, Dr. Laura Schlessinger). My mom loved Dr. Laura's no-nonsense, conservative relationship and family advice. It dovetailed well with the Christian principles espoused in our household. I, on the other hand, bristled at Dr. Laura's caustic way, bossy opinions, and rigid views on the dangers of living together before marriage, mothers who worked outside the home, and divorce. But she was an adult who held a PhD and had a nationwide radio show. Although her words did not feel like truth to me, as a child surrounded by adults who mirrored her messages, it was difficult not to absorb what she was putting down.

In addition to Dr. Laura, I marinated in a stew of Southern culture and evangelical Christianity. By the time I was of marriageable age, I'd been handed a marriage story that included beliefs such as, "The man is the head of the household" and "Divorce is not an option" (unless your husband is an adulterer, an abuser, or an addict – although even if those factors are present, you should stick around as long as you can in hopes of salvaging things). Throw in a few more beliefs such as, "Women do not create wealth; they marry men who do," "It is the man's job to support the family," and "Marriage is hard," and you have a pretty good idea of my marriage story.

Let me be clear here that I mean no disrespect to Dr. Laura or Christianity. I honor whatever teachers, resources, and spiritual path put you in right relationship with yourself and with the higher power of your understanding. The marriage story and its origins are not necessarily the problem, especially if that story resonates with truth for you. The problem comes when the story we've been carrying is no longer our own and interferes with the pursuit of our best life (even if that pursuit means leaving a marriage).

Let me give you an example of what I mean. The Daur people of China's Inner Mongolia have an interesting tradition for couples who want to wed. Before setting a date for their nuptials, the couple must kill a baby chicken together and inspect its liver. If the liver is of healthy condition, they can set a date and the marriage can proceed. However, a liver that is diseased or of poor quality means they cannot yet set a date. They must repeat the process until they find a baby chick with a satisfactory liver.

You may very well be thinking how silly this must seem – how could a chicken liver possibly be relevant to a wedding date or a marriage? But I use this extreme example to illustrate a point. This is a tradition before marriage believed to indicate success of a potential union. The custom is part of this culture's marriage story.

Now, are you nervous that your next friend to get engaged may risk a failed marriage if they don't slaughter and dissect a chicken before picking a date? Probably not. This custom is not a part of your marriage story. But it is for the Daur people. So chicken liver and marriage continue to go hand-in-hand in Inner Mongolia. That, dear reader, is the power of the marriage story that follows us into adulthood.

It may be that your marriage story has you stuck and afraid to move outside its bounds. I am still untangling some aspects of my marriage story to find my own truth, and I'm going to help you do the same. First, however, we need to identify your story.

What Is Your Marriage Story?

You may not be able to readily articulate your marriage story. I didn't realize I had one until I left Tyler behind and began to encounter new and interesting people and professors who had much different views than my own on a myriad of things, including love and relationships.

It's important to note that from birth to about age seven, our brains are in either delta or theta wave state. Of the five categories of brainwaves (i.e., gamma, alpha, beta, theta, and delta) that range from most activity to least activity, delta and theta brainwaves are of the slowest frequency (as a frame of reference, hypnotherapists put their patients in theta wave state for their work). This means that as young children, we are highly suggestible and programmable, much like little sponges for all that goes on around us, including what we absorb about marriage from our family of origin. Throw in about 11 more years of intense family and cultural immersion before most of us leave home at around age 18, and by the time we are adults, we likely have a belief system about most everything in place, including marriage. Once you know that story, you can better decide whether you agree with it or not.

To better help you identify your story, let's get it onto paper. Grab your journal and use the following prompts to tease out your story.

Word Association: The first word that comes to mind when I say marriage is _____.

What my mother, father and/or grandparents said about marriage: _____.

As a child, when I observed the adults around me, I thought this about marriage: _____.

This is just "the way it is" when it comes to marriage: _____.

What I learned about marriage through any religious or spiritual training or curriculum: _____.

What my culture said about marriage: _____.

The book or movie that best portrays my belief on what marriage is like is: _____.

In this book or movie, it says what about marriage: _____.

What I expected marriage to be like: _____.

A feminine role in a marriage consists of what behaviors or actions: _____.

A masculine role in a marriage consists of what behaviors or actions: _____.

Read back over your answers. Are there any common threads? What is the story that emerges from your answers? Based on your responses above, if you had to summarize your marriage story in two or three sentences, please do so in your journal.

Once you've articulated your marriage story above, you may notice that you agree wholeheartedly with this story. It reflects your current values and opinions. If so, that's great! If, however, you are more like me, you may realize that upon taking a closer look at the marriage story overlaid on your life, it feels more like a tight and scratchy piece of clothing – it just doesn't fit. If you are still not quite sure whether your original marriage story fits or not, let's test it against your very own lie detector device: your body.

Your Constant Truth-o-Meter

There is a reason investigators rely on a polygraph test to get to the truth. When the vast majority of humans (save for some sociopaths and psychopaths) tell a lie, there are immediate and automatic physical responses in the body, such as increased perspiration, respiration, heart rate and eye blinking, as well as muscular contractions. So when we say or do something that flies in the face of our truth, whether that be telling a lie or living in such a way that goes against what is true for us, our bodies will react.

I like the way Amy Ahlers, the Wake-Up Call Coach and bestselling author of *Big Fat Lies Women Tell Themselves*, describes it. She explains that when we think of something that causes tension or contraction somewhere in the body, that's usually a sign that it's a big fat lie. In contrast, those light, relaxing, and empowering sensations that come with "Following the Freedom" described in Chapter 4? That, my friend, is an indicator of truth.

Now let's take the marriage story you identified earlier, and put it up against your very own Truth-o-Meter. In other words, we are going to see what your body has to say about this story. To do this, simply sit quietly and allow your answers to rest in your awareness, one at a time. For example, say your mother told you that a difficult marriage was simply a woman's lot in life. Think that thought, "A difficult marriage is simply a woman's lot in life." Does your body feel relaxed, light, and expansive, or does it feel constricted, heavy, or contracted somewhere as you read that statement? A relaxed and expansive bodily feeling likely indicates that your marriage story feels like truth to you – it aligns with who you are.

If, however, your body reacted to the story with contraction and heaviness, that may be a good indicator you are carrying a story that does not reflect your truth – a marriage story that is not your own. It belonged to someone else, like a parent or pastor, they handed it to you, and you may not have realized you didn't have to take it. The thing about a marriage story is that it really should only belong to one person (and if you're lucky, your marriage story may pair well with your spouse's marriage story). The problem comes when other people (be they family, friends, religious leaders, or cultural figures) intrude upon or are involved in your very personal story.

Who Else Is in Your Marriage?

One day you finally knew what you had to do, and began,
though the voices around you kept shouting their bad advice.
MARY OLIVER

I remember vividly the back-and-forth that occurred in my own mind as it became clear that no matter how much therapy my then-husband and I did, no matter how many efforts we made to be kind and reduce the level of conflict between us, my marriage just was not working for me. The immediate internal response was, "But what will *everyone* think if we get divorced?"

The "everyone" in that sentence is an interesting word. To me at the time, it encompassed the whole world. It felt like me versus this sea of faces, all frowning in disapproval and disappointment if I were to announce my separation. In sociological terms, this is called the "generalized other." It refers to an individual's internalized impression of societal norms and expectations. Interestingly, what we don't realize is that "everyone" does not actually encompass the whole world.

Instead, it likely represents the voice of just one or two people who played a prominent role in our formative years. As I drilled down on this voice in my own life, I quickly came to realize that the voice of my "everyone" was made up of several particularly critical mothers of childhood friends for whom money and social status meant the world. My divorce would mean (in my mind, anyway) that I was leaving behind my affluent lifestyle and would be looked down upon and criticized.

So here I was in my mid-30s, extremely unhappy in my marriage, yet on some level staying put partly because I was afraid of what several long ago, far away women from my childhood would think. Once I learned about the "generalized other," I realized just how banana pancakes this was! In reality, these women would likely never give me and my divorce a second thought. And if they did? Truthfully their opinions were completely irrelevant to my best life.

Now I would invite you to explore who else might be involved in your marriage, keeping you stuck and scared? Who is the "everyone" in your relationship? Who are those people whose criticism and reaction you fear the most? If you are having a hard time identifying this person or persons, just look back at your responses above. Whose voice is the loudest, the most judgmental? From whom do you least want to risk disapproval or who do you least want to disappoint?

Once you've identified this person or persons, ask yourself whether you want them in your marriage story. Have they earned the right to be there? Do they have your best interest at heart? Do their values and opinions align with your own? If the answer is yes to these questions, that's awesome!

If, however, you don't want these folks crowding around your marriage bed, figuratively taking up space in your guest room, and offering unsolicited advice on how to proceed in your relationship, then keep reading. The good news is that now is your chance to eliminate the "everyone" from your marriage and trade your old marriage story for a new story – a story that aligns perfectly with your unique core values and belief system.

A Marriage Story to Call Your Own

Angela is a working mother of three boys who came to see me after she separated from her husband. She is bright, funny, and kind, and has done quite well as an executive at a tech company. After 20 years of marriage, Angela knew it was time to end things and she felt good about her decision. The one problem was those pesky thoughts that were keeping her up at night.

Angela is the primary breadwinner for her family. She carries enormous guilt over how her soon-to-be ex-husband will fare without her support. And what about her boys? She fears that her divorce will affect her children negatively, making her a bad mother for leaving.

That's where I come in. One of my primary jobs as a coach is to help my clients question their painful and limiting thoughts – the ones that keep them in fear and prevent them from moving forward. I know a lot about beliefs such as these. I had a ton of them circulating in my own head as I decided how to proceed in my marriage. Thoughts like, "My family and friends will be disappointed in me," and "I will never be able to support myself in the same way my husband provided for us" played constantly in my mind.

At the time, I didn't have the benefit of incredibly effective coaching tools to help me deal with these scary thoughts. Instead, I simply waited until the pain of staying put exceeded my fear of the unknown, and I leapt. That's an okay way to do it – in fact, that's one of the primary questions I ask clients to help with the "should I stay or should I go?" dilemma.

There is a better way, however. There are some amazing tools to help you make your decision from a place of clarity and peace, not confusion and anxiety. I'm going to share some of them with you here.

Your Thoughts Are Not the Boss of You

We are disturbed not by what happens to us, but by our thoughts about what happens.
EPICTETUS, Greek philosopher

As humans, we have around 60,000 – 80,000 thoughts per day, the vast majority of which are negative, and many of them are repeats. However, these thoughts often feel incredibly real, true, and relevant.

Take for instance the story of my first real boyfriend in high school. We dated for a year before leaving for different colleges. When long-distance just wasn't cutting it, the demise of our young love seemed imminent. My thought at the time was, "If he breaks up with me, my life will be ruined."

Oh my goodness, did this thought feel so real! I spent weeks crying and ruminating over what my life would be like without him. I truly believed everything would go up in flames if we were to breakup. Perhaps you can relate? Not surprisingly, he did break up with me. The days that followed were mighty painful. Lots of hot tears, grief, and a certainty that I'd never find a love like that again.

Yet here I sit today, surrounded by a wonderful life and my heart more filled with love than I ever could have imagined. Lo and behold, my life was not ruined! That was merely a thought. The fact that the breakup of a high school relationship might not even be painful for some teens further underscores why this was *just a thought*. Who knows, that same breakup might even have been liberating for someone else. I think the Greek philosopher Epictetus was onto something when he so astutely observed that, "We are disturbed not by what happens to us, but by our thoughts about what happens."

What to Do with All Those Pesky Thoughts

I just know that whenever I am being my mind's b*tch, I am not living in my natural state of joy. I am not living my Truth, which is that I am already free and infinite.
PAM GROUT, *Thank & Grow Rich*

So if it's our thoughts about what happens and not what actually happens that's the issue, what's a gal to do? The answer is to question the heck out of those painful thoughts to determine whether they are actually true. Like a detective interrogating a suspect, you gotta get to the truth, to the real story.

My preferred method for doing so comes from Byron Katie, in my opinion, one of the greatest spiritual teachers and masters of our time. After a transcendent experience in the late 1980s, Katie developed a system of inquiry called *The Work* that allows you to explore whether your most painful thoughts are actually true.

Although it may seem counter-intuitive, the opposite of our painful thoughts are often as true or perhaps even truer than the original thought. Take my belief about my high school boyfriend that, "If he breaks up with me, my life will be ruined." Clearly not true. But what about the opposite: "If he breaks up with me, my life may just be beginning." Now that was the truth!

Taking this line of reasoning a step further, if the opposite of our painful thoughts might just be true, what if these painful thoughts were less of a torture device and more of a benevolent alarm system alerting us to unnecessary suffering? Put another way, our most uncomfortable nagging thoughts and the suffering that accompanies them might just be a broadcast system of sorts that is calling us home to ourselves to consider and examine what is really true for us.

Let's return to Angela's story as an example. One of her worrisome thoughts was, "I need to take care of my husband." But is this thought actually true? It certainly felt true for Angela. I encouraged her to put the thought under the interrogator's spotlight and explore whether the opposite might be as true or truer.

We turned this thought on its head in several different ways. It first became: "I do not need to take care of my husband." I asked her if she could come up with several reasons why this new thought might be true. She replied that she didn't need to take care of him because he was a capable adult, he took care of himself before they were married, and he had degrees and training that would certainly serve him well in his chosen work now.

As we continued our exploration, more new thoughts occurred to her, such as maybe she was actually doing him a disservice by continuing to take care of him. In fact, she'd noticed that he'd become somewhat unfulfilled and apathetic as of late. Perhaps if she wasn't taking care of him, he might finally have the impetus and motivation to dive into meaningful work that would give his life more purpose. Now Angela was starting to feel some serious relief!

We looked around for other variations of her original painful thought to see whether we could increase her relief and clarity, and came up with a few more. Namely, the thought could become, "My husband needs to take care of himself."

Was it possible this might be true? Absolutely! And the clincher that really brought the exercise home? Angela turned it back on herself for the whopping realization that, "I need to take care of myself." Whoa. After a lifetime of caring for everyone *but* herself, the weight of truth in this statement stopped her in her tracks.

Just in case these mental thought gymnastics aren't cutting it for you, remember there's always another failsafe to finding truth: your body. Just "Follow the Freedom" toward the best feeling (i.e., truest) thought. When I asked Angela which felt more free between her original thought (i.e., "I need to take care of my husband") and its opposite (i.e., "I do not need to take care of my husband"), the answer was clear. The thought that she had to take care of him caused an undeniable physical reaction. Her chest became tight and her throat clenched uncomfortably, indicating we were in big fat lie territory. So we leaned into the better-feeling thought, the one that empowered her and brought her peace. Simply thinking the thought, "I do not need to take care of my husband" softened her chest and throat and she felt immediate relief. Her body had spoken and the message was clear.

As we concluded our session, Angela had experienced a reprieve from the painful thought loop that had been playing on repeat in her head and keeping her stuck. She could now make her decision from a place of fearless clarity and wisdom, instead of fear-based confusion and self-blame.

As any neuroscientist will tell you, what fires together wires together. If we allow ourselves to keep thinking the same painful (and likely untrue) thought over and over, that is the neural pathway working a well-worn rut in our brain. However, if we allow for the possibility of a new story, one that may very well be as true or truer than the original, we are building new neural pathways that can become a foundation for new experiences, growth, and an awesome new life.

The Playlist You Need to Delete

Chances are you have some song playlists on your various devices you need to delete. Maybe those tunes are simply old and just aren't doing it for you anymore, or maybe when they come on you want to put a fork in your ear. In much the same way, you likely have some thoughts and fears about your marriage that are no longer serving you. Time to create a new mental playlist.

First, let's capture those limiting beliefs that are keeping you paralyzed in fear. If you don't already know the playlist that's been on repeat, try using the following prompts:

If I were to get divorced, this would happen: _____.

If I were to get divorced, this is what my family and friends would think: _____.

If I were to get divorced, I am afraid my life would change in this way: _____.

If I were to get divorced, my kids would: _____.

If I were to get divorced, I would lose: _____.

If I were to get divorced, it would have the following financial effect: _____.

If I were to get divorced, this would be harder: _____.

If I were to get divorced, I fear that: _____.

Read back over your answers. What do you notice? Are there any common threads? Are there any surprises?

Now let's take those thoughts put them under the interrogation spotlight, in much the same way I did with my client Angela. Say for example, one of your fears is that "If I were to get divorced, my kids would be damaged." That might be true. But let's explore whether there could be another possibility by turning it around and feeling for truth.

Flipped to the opposite, the thought might become, "If I were to get divorced, my kids would be healed." Can you find a reason that could be true? Maybe your marriage is super-high-conflict, as mine was. You are fairly certain your kids are feeling the effects of all that fighting. Transitioning to two peaceful divorced parents in two loving, low-conflict homes might actually be an improvement. And double-check it against your Truth-o-Meter: Which thought feels more free and expansive in your body, and which one feels like a big fat lie?

Or perhaps your thought was, "If I were to get divorced, I will never find love again." Turn it around, and it could become, "If I were to get divorced, I may find greater love than I had before." And to build those new neural pathways, explore why this might this be possible. Perhaps because now you know what works and what doesn't in a relationship; you are wiser and have the benefit of years of relationship experience; and because you have honed your preferences over time. Now double-check it with your body. Which thought feels more like freedom?

I invite you to take each of your fill-in-the-blank statements above and put them under the interrogation spotlight. Don't let these suspect thoughts jerk you around without getting to the truth. And for those thoughts that reek of untruth, question the heck out of them and then delete them from your playlist. Your fearful, painful thoughts do not have to be the boss of you, and they do not need to play on repeat. Encourage, nourish, and go toward the freedom thoughts, the ones that support your most empowered and expansive life.

What If You Can't Even Bring Yourself to Say the "D" Word?

I used to envision quite frequently what my life would look like if I were to leave my marriage. I wondered what it would be like to feel the peace that comes from not living in a constant state of marital turmoil. I imagined what it would feel like to be financially independent, the bottom line in making big decisions.

But maybe you aren't quite ready to envision divorce. Maybe you haven't admitted, even to yourself, where an unhappy marriage might lead. The only way to move forward, however, is to look the dirtiest, scariest, ugliest parts square in the eye. What you find may surprise you, much like the story of the revered Tibetan yogi Milarepa.

As the legend goes, one day Milarepa returned to his cave dwelling only to find it filled with demons. After several failed attempts to get them out through force, then cajoling, then teaching them a few spiritual principles, he finally resigned himself to living with them, at which point all but one of the demons disappeared. The remaining demon was pretty freaking scary, the most intimidating of them all. Surrendering even further, old Milarepa offered himself up to the demon, placing his head into its gaping maw. And the demon then dissolved into the ethers.

It's easy to spend years trying to hide from the scariest fears about potentially ending your marriage. But I encourage you to surrender yourself to them, at least long enough to explore whether they might not be as real as you think. And when you do, you may find that they dissolve into nothingness, leaving you free to make decisions about your future from a place of wisdom and clarity.

You're Not Confused, Promise

One of the most common statements repeated in my office is some variation of, "I don't know whether to stay or go – I'm just so confused." My response may sound a little harsh, but we've been through several chapters together by now, so I think you can handle it. I'm going to call you on your confusion and throw a hunch: You are not confused about what to do; you are afraid of the action you know you must take.

I've been there. I used to say I was confused. But in the depths of my heart, I knew that I was in the wrong marriage and I needed to get out. It just took me several years to get to the point where I could acknowledge and do something about it.

There is no rush, dear reader, to let go of the idea of confusion and move forward into scary choices and actions. In fact, I always advise clients to stay until they absolutely know that they know. Although I chose to end my marriage, I want to pause here and point out that the ramifications of divorce are no joke and should not be taken lightly. While I am resolute and unwavering in my decision to leave, I nevertheless experienced extreme grief and guilt along the way. It is a small but powerful salve during any post-divorce pain to feel confident that you did everything you could to salvage the relationship.

One quick caveat here: If you are involved with an abuser, a narcissist, a sociopath, or a psychopath, then in my book, all bets are off, and you have my full blessing to get out of Dodge ASAP. Much more essential than my blessing, however, is the permission *you* must give yourself to walk away from such a relationship.

As this chapter on marriage stories and painful, fearful thoughts comes to a close, I will leave you with one final question, knowing that you absolutely can stay in confusion and stagnation as long as you want: What is the story you want to write for yourself? The story you want your kids, family, and friends to tell about you? That you stayed a lifetime in an unhappy but tolerable marriage ... or that you bravely followed your heart and truth to create a life that honors the deepest, realest parts of you?

Perhaps the story you wish to tell at the end of your life involves making some scary choices and acting with courage. If so, and you're feeling a bit overwhelmed by all these emotions, never fear! The chapter that follows will get you ready to feel all those feels in a safe, approachable way.

CHAPTER 6
Feeling All the Feels

Bottled-up feelings burn and rarely come out tasting good –
think vomit-flavored Sriracha.
Scott Stabile, *Big Love*

Just several years ago, I was living from the neck up. I prided myself on operating from my rational brain while squelching all those pesky and supposedly negative emotions like sadness, anger, or grief. They always seemed like a huge inconvenience, a sign of weakness, and a big ol' waste of time. My stint as an overwhelmed young associate at a large law firm reinforced this line of thinking.

I believed that I could shut off my unwanted emotions and steel myself against any chance of another person affecting me negatively. This idea gave me a (false) sense of power and security. I told myself there was no room for hurt if there was no vulnerability. I guess my strategy could have worked if I were a robot. But that's the thing about being human. We are physiologically wired to *feel* things. Whether or not I wanted to have my feelings, they were still happening in my body. To be completely honest, I had a sneaking suspicion I actually felt things quite intensely, both my own pain and that of others. But I just continued to stuff all those emotions down. And the internal time bomb continued to grow.

Then came my marriage. Jesus Christ on a cracker, my husband knew how to push my buttons. For the first time in my life, I could not tamp my feelings down any longer. My husband incited reactions out of me that I did not think were possible. It was like throwing a lit match into a vat of kerosene. God forbid I miss a day of the birth control pills I was taking at the time. Once I'd realized my mistake and took two pills the following day, doubling up on those tiny hormone firecrackers seemed to take my anger to what felt like homicidal levels. Not too long ago, my ex even revealed he almost hid our cutlery after watching one too many episodes of *Wives with Knives* while we were teetering on the brink of divorce. Probably not a bad call.

My anger felt so hot, my insides like a balloon about to burst. I would catch myself making fists so tight that my fingernails could almost draw blood against my palms. I instituted a practice that I called "running the rage" on our local hike-and-bike trail. To run was the only way I knew how to keep from what felt like a literal explosion. This practice helped, but I began to suspect that my anger was merely a symptom, a clue seeping out that begged me to look closer.

After replacing a phone I shattered into pieces after throwing it against a wall in a moment of rage, I had to admit there was more going in my body than I'd let myself acknowledge previously. This kind of reaction could not arise in a vacuum. I feared there was a toxicity rooted in the depths of my being, but

I still wasn't quite ready to poke around in this unfamiliar and scary territory just yet.

Instead, I made a conscious decision to do an emotional checkout of sorts in my marriage. As opposed to engaging with my husband, I would look to my friends to fill the need for connection. If I drank, the first couple glasses of wine could soften the wall I'd put between us and allow me to appreciate my husband's role in providing such an amazing life for us (by glass four or five, however, the anger often returned tenfold ... but I rarely factored that in when reaching for my constant companion, Prosecco).

Separate bedrooms and second homes provided just enough distance so the lit match didn't really reach the kerosene all that often anymore. This strategy worked for a while, but frankly it was exhausting and unfulfilling. More importantly, it was a flimsy veneer of inauthenticity that began to grate against my Wise Authentic Self, whose whispers were now becoming a roar.

The Bucket and the Cinder Block

I sat down across the couch from my therapist. I was now eight years into my relationship. This was the same therapist I'd seen for couples counseling in year one of my marriage. We'd carried a bucket full of hurts and resentments down the aisle with us and it had to be dealt with. In fact, to this post-divorce day, we call these issues (some were resolved, others weren't) our Bucket Issues. Oh, how I hated that damn bucket.

We seemed unable to communicate effectively or constructively on our own, and the bucket was overflowing. So to therapy we went, my husband with his therapist and me with mine, additionally coming together regularly to meet jointly as a group of four. Then my husband unilaterally quit couples therapy. It is no exaggeration to say I was devastated. And enraged. It was the only place I ever felt heard or received any validation that I wasn't losing my ever-loving mind amidst the fighting.

I'd held onto my therapist's number during those in-between years where I was able to drink enough booze and take enough trips with my girlfriends to stay somewhat delightfully fun and numb. Around 2010, however, the cracks in my perfect life were beginning to show, and my husband and I agreed that it would be in everyone's best interest if I were to get a little support.

So there I sat across from my therapist with my arms crossed over my chest, per usual. I will never forget the session when she gently suggested that I uncross my arms. Begrudgingly I did. I hadn't realized how much safer I felt with the barrier of my arms protecting my body. Then she asked me to take a deep breath. I did. She asked, "What's going on in your chest?" My initial reaction was confusion. What do you mean "going on in my chest?" She pushed further, and asked me whether the area around my heart felt tight. Holy mother of God, it did! How had I not realized this?

She prodded a bit more, all the while encouraging me to breathe gently but deeply. Crap, there was a freaking cinder block in there! How did that get there, and how had I not noticed it before? Those thoughts quickly disappeared, however, as I involuntarily collapsed into gasping sobs.

The mind-body perimeter had been breached, the area below my neck had been acknowledged, and there was no turning back. I surrendered to the frustrating and disappointing realization that I had emotions that I'd apparently been carrying for quite some time, all neatly compressed and compacted into a block in my chest. Fortunately, as both my therapy and divorce progressed, the block in my chest began to loosen.

Don't Suck It Up, Buttercup!

I later learned that our emotions are simply energy in motion, and our bodies are the container for this cascade of chemical and physiological reactions. If you don't allow them to move through you as they are designed to, they get stored in the body. If you've found yourself stuck and scared in an unhappy marriage, you, too, may have some emotions you've been avoiding. You may not be carrying them as a cinder block in your chest, but chances are, they're in there somewhere.

As humans, we tend to suppress unwanted emotions through shallow breathing and muscular tension. For example, recall a moment in public when tears began to well up. Maybe the in-flight movie on that crowded airplane brought it on. Or a conversation at a cocktail party prompted a wave of grief following the loss of your beloved animal companion. Or, as was frequent for me and my ex, you got in a fight with your spouse in a packed restaurant and you just couldn't keep from breaking down. Regardless of the trigger, if you perceive that crying is not appropriate at the moment, what do you do? You suck it up.

There is a reason it's called "sucking it up." It's an inhale to suck it all back in. You call back the tears and quickly blot away any that had a chance to escape. You try to tame the irregular gulping sobs into calm and orderly breathing. You steel yourself against the tidal wave of emotion and tighten your body and face into some semblance of composure. You stuff whatever was trying to come out into a recess of your being. If this happens every so often, but you actually make a point to return for these feelings and they have a chance to move on through, that is not so much of a problem.

However, if your regular MO is to send every unwanted emotion into an internal storage unit with a tight, heavy lid, *that* can become problematic. The squelched intensity of repressed emotions such as despair, rage, and worry can then cause all kinds of fun physiological problems (e.g., compulsions, psychosomatic illnesses, addictions, insomnia and neuroses, just to name a few).

The emotions you ignore become like children. Your little neglected emo children. Have you ever attempted to ignore a whiny three-year old tugging at your pant leg? It's not pretty. You can usually depend on them getting louder and more insistent until they receive the attention they are demanding. And your emo children are no different.

Like actual children, when ignored and suppressed emotions do start to seep out, you often have little control over them, and it usually happens at the most inopportune of times, like a holiday party when you are a bit over-served and your inhibitions are down, or a meeting at work when you just can't hold your frustration at a bullying boss any longer. Of course, you can turn to the usual suspects for numbing and distraction (e.g., drinking, prescription or recreational drugs, shopping, gambling, or endless hours on social media and Netflix). These quick fixes may quiet your emo children temporarily, but numb and distract all you want, those kids are still going to be there staring at you when you sober up and come back to reality.

In addition to the repercussions of repression, it's also true that you can't just pick and choose your emotions. In other words, closing yourself off from fear and sadness, for example, means you are closing yourself off from real joy and happiness, as well. Bottom line, despite your best efforts to negate them, if you are human, you will have emotions, and the detrimental consequences of not feeling them are well-documented. Instead, take care of your little emos, and you will greatly enhance the quality of your life and your general sense of well-being.

Feeling All the Feels

Susan sat across from me in my office. She reminded me a lot of myself several years prior. She definitely appeared to have it all together and her life looked pretty damn perfect from the outside. She and her husband fell into the power couple category. Two multi-six-figure incomes, a beautiful house, cute children. They seemed to have it all.

Underneath the surface, however, there was an undercurrent of extreme dissatisfaction. Marital and work resentments were easy to access, as was grief over a loss suffered several years prior. But Susan didn't want to spend much time there. She was afraid that if she looked too closely, it would be like opening Pandora's Box. She would be consumed with her difficult emotions and she'd never be able to close that damn box and get anything done from her massive list of personal and professional responsibilities. She feared she would be unable to maintain her well-appointed and orderly life while dealing with the messiness of her unruly emotions.

That's the thing about emotions, though – they are designed to move like a waterfall through the body. Unobstructed, they will simply flow right on through, and your body will return to stasis in short order. But don't just take my word for it. Dr. Jill Bolte Taylor is a neuroscientist who suffered a stroke in her mid-30s that took her left-brain language center completely offline for a period of months. During her recovery, she found that an emotion, unimpeded by the narrative created by our left-brain (like whether the emotion should be happening, whether it is an inconvenient time to be experiencing the emotion, or whether we're going crazy), will flow right through us in about 90 seconds. In fact, she said she could set her watch by these 90-second intervals.

So what does it actually mean to feel your emotions, to let them pass through you like a waterfall? For many years, I was not very adept at this. In fact, it was not until I entered life coach training that I really made any commitment to doing this at all. The good news is that I will share a little secret I learned there that will allow you to hit the ground running as you begin to embrace your emotions.

Just Breathe

The big secret to feeling your emotions? Just breathe. Yep, it's that simple. Remember earlier when I mentioned that humans tend to suppress emotions through muscular tension and shallow breathing? To allow for emotions, simply do the opposite. And that's exactly what I did: I breathed deeply and threw off the tight, heavy lid.

Now it's your turn to try this exercise. Consciously relax your whole body while keeping your awareness in your body, not your thoughts in your head (an easy way to do this is to place your hand gently over your heart or some other part of the body, as that stimulates the neurons in that area, making it easier to keep your attention there). Also, try to avoid distractions as best you can. Then focus on breathing deeply and restfully for about five minutes. That's all there is to it.

When I first started doing this exercise, inevitably I'd end up in an ugly cry in about 30 seconds. Over time, however, the crying jags subsided as my body released what I had previously suppressed. Things improved even more when I started to actually feel my emotions as they came up in my day-to-day life (as opposed to denying their existence and pushing them into a shadowy recess of my being).

That means, for example, when I feel a wave of grief cresting for what seems like the umpteen-millionth time since my beloved kitty companion passed several months ago, instead of internally chastising myself for not being over it by now, I lean into it. I simply acknowledge the emotion that I'm feeling without judgment. I then evaluate whether there is an action I want to take, and I give myself space to respond. With the grief, for example, I might allow myself the space to withdraw and cry.

Or when I feel a surge of anger, I might run my rage to burn off the initial adrenaline burst, and then look into what caused it. Perhaps there is an injustice to be righted, or I've allowed a violation of my boundaries. If all else fails, I can always head over to Goodwill and buy some cheap plates that I can ever-so-satisfyingly break on the big slab of concrete in my backyard (fortunately, my neighbors are quite tolerant of my rituals).

Bottom line, there is no right way to feel your emotions. All that is required is the awareness that they're happening and the allowance of space in your body for your little emo children to be present. Follow what you feel led to do with them. Cry when the tears well up. Speak your truth to right an injustice. Rest when grief incapacitates you. And that is how you feel all the feels.

Your Emotions = Waze for Your Life

Have you ever used the community-based traffic and navigation app, Waze? It provides real-time traffic and road info, alerting you before you approach speed traps, accidents, or road hazards, and it helps you outsmart traffic jams. It's basically a friendly heads-up for your best driving routes as you navigate your day.

In much the same way, your emotions are like Waze for your life, except this app conveniently comes automatically downloaded into your being from birth. Your emotions are like the interface between the outside world and your Wise Authentic Self. They are a source of information and a guidance system akin to a compass.

We often embrace the positive emotions, like joy, contentment, and compassion. They're a pretty good indicator that we're heading in the direction of our best life. The emotions that most consider negative, like anger, sadness, and grief, however, usually garner different responses. Those are the ones with a bad rap that many people try to dodge.

But what if, instead of a nuisance to be avoided or suppressed, these emotions were a tool designed to let us know when something is off in our life? Of course when you lose a loved one, for example, intense sadness and grief are a natural response. That's what we would call "clean pain." If, however, you have a continuous bodily reaction of anxiety that accompanies you every day at your job, or depression that stems from your relationship, these may be reliable indicators that something is amiss and needs to be addressed. While it comes packaged in an emotion that might feel pretty uncomfortable, it can actually be an incredible gift. Before I lose you to a Liz Lemon-style epic eye roll at the notion of rage or sadness as a gift, let me explain what I mean.

When my client Jenny came to see me for the first time, she was quite sure she needed to leave her marriage. After the birth of her first child, she and her spouse had grown apart. They no longer slept in the same bed, they shared very little in common, and while my client was in the middle of a spiritual awakening of sorts, her spouse had little interest in growing or expanding in such a way. Perhaps these things would have been tolerable, but unfortunately, her spouse was quite critical, to boot. He was like an albatross determined to bring her down as she rose like a buoy to greater levels of awareness and joy. For Jenny, all of this resulted in what Karla McLaren, emotion researcher and empathy pioneer, calls "situational depression."

Defined as a low mood that tracks to something you can affect with changes to your lifestyle or behavior, it differs from the more intense forms of clinical depression, which may require therapeutic and/or medical intervention. McLaren actually calls such situational depression "The Ingenious Stop Sign of the Soul." She notes that it arises when some aspect of your life is already unworkable or dysfunctional. In Jenny's case, her low mood tracked closely to her relationship. She ultimately decided to leave her marriage. While the journey out was not all sunshine and roses, now several years later, she is thriving and no longer experiencing the low mood that followed her for the final years of her marriage.

Jenny could have simply ignored or suppressed her situational depression. Instead, however, she was able to view it as a sign from her Wise Authentic Self. Taking the cue from that sign directed her out of an unhealthy marriage and into the life she really wanted to be living. In this way, her emotions became a gift, signaling where she needed to go.

You might be wondering why your soul has to speak in such uncomfortable terms sometimes. You might even promise to cave earlier and listen sooner, before the anxiety, the sadness, and the anger reach a breaking point. But let's be honest, if some of the more important emotions didn't create a bit of suffering or discomfort, would they really grab your attention and would you really spend your already-precious time processing them and making necessary life changes?

Some of your most uncomfortable emotions may actually be your Wise Authentic Self's way of getting your attention in an attempt to redirect you back to the path of your best life. If that is true, and the whole spectrum of your emotions are each gifts in their own unique way, what might they each be trying to tell you about your marriage?

CHAPTER 7

The Selfless Act
of Self-Love

You are not in need of self-help; you are in need of self-love.
AMY B. SCHER, author of *How to Heal Yourself When No One Else Can*

I'm Third

Every summer from ages 10 through 18, I spent a month at a Christian athletics camp in the Ozark Mountains of Missouri. We sang corny songs, played a variety of sports, and went on wilderness adventures, all with a heavy overlay of fundamentalist Christian theology. At the end of the month when parents arrived to claim their kids, there were track and swim meets, family picnics, and the all-important closing ceremony where individual camper awards were given.

The final honor bestowed upon one lucky camper every year was the "I'm Third" award. It was the most prestigious and coveted award. It honored the founder and original director of the camp, as well as a pilot from the 1950s who heroically refused to bail out of his crippled plane during an airshow. By going down with his plane, he was able to maneuver around the houses and people below, and crash in the only empty plot of land around, thereby preventing any deaths other than his own.

I heard this story of the courageous pilot many times during my years at this camp. He received a great deal of praise because he so beautifully exemplified the "I'm Third" motto of "God first, the other person second, and I'm third." The camp taught that this was the best way, nay the only way, to live. For many years, I believed them.

I took those words to heart. I tried to live them. But time and again I just ended up feeling like the crud underneath the bottom of the Jesus sandals I used to imagine a judgy male God with long white hair wore from his throne on high. Lived literally, I always came last – if God is first, and others come second, then who else is left at the end of the line but me?

As the last person standing there, it was difficult not to question my inherent worth and value (especially when I'd already been told I was flawed, incomplete, and destined for Hell without acceptance of Christ as my personal savior). After a certain point, I instead began to question the dogma through a careful, historical study of the origins of Christianity and the Bible. Much like my marriage story, perhaps this religious story was not mine, either.

Please note it is not my intention to single out Christianity for a beat-down in this book. Christianity was simply one of the lenses through which much of my early life was framed. I also realize that the particular version of this religion presented to me was on the more conservative side of the faith, and I no longer believe it is an accurate reflection of the true life or message of Jesus Christ.

My intention is, however, to highlight the fact that many faiths, cultural traditions, and stories from our families of origin provide messaging that others' needs come before our own. Case in point, the oft-repeated phrase, "It is better to give than receive" transcends multiple religious and cultural traditions. Making the whole issue even thornier, females are usually the ones to bear the brunt of this messaging. Again, despite faith or geography, women regularly learn from an early age that it is our job to be the caretakers of everyone and everything around us.

Don't get me wrong, I still love the story of the brave pilot who gave his life for others. I hope I would do the same in a similar situation. What I do not love, however, is the effect that "I'm Third" motto had on me as I grew and developed my sense of self-worth and my relationships with others. You may also have had your own version of an "I'm Third" story that affected you, as well.

For me, the result of living the "I'm Third" principle for many formative years manifested in several ways by the time I hit adulthood. I lived much of my life in apology energy. I found myself saying, "I'm sorry" for virtually everything. If a distracted stranger glued to their phone bumped into me on the sidewalk? "I'm sorry." Or if I had more items in my cart than the person behind me in line at Whole Foods and I knew checkout would take a while? "I'm sorry." Or if a server at my favorite restaurant brought me the wrong meal and I needed to correct the error? "I'm sorry." It began to seem like I was apologizing for my very existence, for taking up space that I felt belonged more rightfully to others.

I also was virtually unable to say no when someone asked something of me. Join your committee that I have no interest in or time for? "Sure!" Cancel my longstanding dinner plans so I can finish that work project for you? "You got it!" Sit in an hour of traffic to attend that boring party with you so you won't have to go by yourself? "I'd love to!" Others' needs ahead of mine!

I deferred to others in making choices about movies to see, restaurants to try, or just about anything where preferences were involved. Although I had an opinion about nearly all of this stuff, I doubt anyone ever knew it. I was a people-pleaser extraordinaire and came across as pleasant and easygoing. The needs and wants of others always trumped my own. "I'm Third" – it's the only way to live!

After years of putting myself last, I was a shell of a person – an angry, resentful, exhausted shell. I had given and given and given, and my cup no longer ranneth over. It was bone dry. Additionally, my receiving muscle had totally atrophied. I was unable to accept compliments, love, support, or compensation. I demurred, deflected, and denied it all.

By this point, I'd already given up on God liking me – the Christianity of my youth no longer felt like truth to me, and I certainly wasn't living in accordance with the dictates of the faith. It would be several years before I rekindled my relationship with the Divine through more spiritual avenues. In the meantime, because I felt so crappy and unworthy on the inside, I turned to the outside world for validation.

From my vantage point, the most revered, valued, and adored members of our society appeared to be those who were either beautiful, smart, or wealthy. If you were all three, even better. So I spent the next 15 years trying to embody that sham of a trifecta. Through extreme dieting and exercise, plastic surgery, and drugs, I attempted to mold my face and body into that of a *Playboy* centerfold. I spent several years getting a graduate degree in law to prove I was smart. And I married a powerful man who provided great wealth, the ultimate insulation and protection from a scary world.

And after achieving it all, I found that I still felt incredibly empty inside. I feared I would be nothing if you took away the armor of externals. Little did I know that the missing component among all of this madness, the thing that would resolve almost all of my issues, was self-love.

So Damn Thirsty

Love is our most important business, and any love we give
ourselves is love that serves us all.
Scott Stabile, *Big Love*

When I left my marriage, I wasn't sure where I was headed. All I had was an amorphous and poorly-formed idea of moving back to the West Coast and, after a brief sabbatical from my entire life, the notion of helping real people one-on-one in any area but law. Through a serendipitous and unexpected turn of events, I entered life coach training.

To this day, the word "life coach" makes me gag a little. Despite my misgivings about the label, however, I couldn't deny my love for everything I was learning about neuroscience, personal growth, positive psychology, and spirituality. I had been bone dry for so long. I was, as the Persian poet Hafiz so eloquently put it, "so damn thirsty."

I also knew that what I'd been doing wasn't working. I had been given the unique opportunity to have just about everything our culture tells us will make us happy. And while I won't say I was miserable – my happiness thermostat setting is naturally pretty high, not to mention my problems were decidedly First World – I had been profoundly unfulfilled. I was ready to try just about anything, from psychedelic journeys using plant medicine to metaphysical conferences, and even (gasp!) life coaching.

While I embraced many of the concepts I was learning, there was one that just didn't resonate for me: self-love. I usually rolled my eyes (at least internally) at the folks selling that snake oil. I wrote them off as indulgent self-help junkies. The word came up often in the coaching and spiritual circles I ran in. But it had no weight, no substance. It was overused, fluffy, and meaningless to me. Besides, I was an attorney. What self-respecting attorney (albeit not practicing) could peddle self-love?

I couldn't deny, however, how good it felt to be nice to myself. Sure, it was awkward at first, attempting to offer myself love and compassion against the backdrop of the shrill voice of my inner critic, who had a bad habit of screaming about the size of my thighs or how no one would like me if I no longer had a fancy vacation home in Hollywood. But with practice, I began to see shifts.

I could tell, for instance, that my self-critical thoughts (e.g., "You fat pig – look at how much weight you've gained!" or "You are nothing without your husband's money") made me feel tight and crunchy inside. Cue the big fat lie alarm! More supportive thoughts, however (e.g., "Look at how much you've accomplished despite starting over completely" or "You have so much to offer the world"), felt light and expansive. They felt like … you guessed it, freedom!

While I wasn't levitating through life emanating self-love just yet, I suspected that this concept might just be the key component I'd been missing to unlocking my best life. So I continued to follow the freedom and practice self-love as best I could, all of which led me to Anita Moorjani, a near-death experience (NDE) survivor, bestselling author, and my newfound personal self-love hero.

Myth Busters: Loving Yourself is Selfish

Loving ourselves is actually the most important thing we can do – it's the key to living a blissful life.
ANITA MOORJANI, *What If THIS Is Heaven?*

"For our last exercise of the evening, I would like to go around the circle and have each of you share three positive traits about yourself," I said to the women in the book club I was facilitating at a local Seattle bookshop. We were wrapping up a lively discussion exploring the myth that loving yourself is selfish. The women surrounding me were all intelligent, entertaining, articulate, and well-read. I could have quickly and easily named a handful of amazing qualities about each one of them. Yet the group looked at me like deer caught in the headlights. If I were a mind reader, my hunch is the collective internal response was something along the lines of, "Oh, crap – does she seriously expect us to do this?"

As we proceeded to go around the circle one-by-one and share our answers, I was struck by how difficult this exercise was for us. We had a hard time coming up with a whopping three whole traits. We qualified our responses (e.g., "I write well" quickly followed by "I mean, I'm not a writer...."). I personally had to make a verbal commitment to the group to actually look them in the eye while sharing my traits – it was soooo uncomfortable!

It was a simple exercise suggested in the book we were discussing, *What If THIS Is Heaven?* Authored by Anita Moorjani, it explores the top cultural myths that keep us from experiencing heaven on earth, one of which she posits is "loving yourself is selfish." I myself had fallen prey to this myth. Who had time for the arrogance and audacity of self-love if I was supposed to be putting myself third all the time? Although Anita was raised Hindu, she had received similar dogmatic religious messaging, and she had little love of self. That is, until she had the mother of all near-death experiences.

After four years with lymphoma, Anita was losing her battle with cancer. Her emaciated body was riddled with lemon-sized tumors that protruded from her 85 lb frame. She had lesions covering her body that oozed with the toxins her overwhelmed and failing organs could no longer process. In February 2006, she finally slipped into a coma and doctors notified her family she would die very soon. But she didn't.

Instead, she went to that ineffable place of light described by most all NDE survivors, including my friend Tara, who you met in Chapter 4. There, Anita encountered loved ones who had passed on before her, and she experienced the most beautiful, unconditional love she had ever felt. Following her NDE, with her family and doctors in stunned disbelief, her organs began to function again and she woke up. Even more miraculous, in less than a week, her tumors had shrunk by approximately 70 percent. Within about a month, she walked away from the hospital and her astonished doctors without a trace of cancer in her body.

My brief synopsis here does not begin to do her story true justice – it is just the tip of the iceberg in terms of the unbelievable events that went down. But I include it here because one of the biggest revelations Anita returned with is the knowledge that loving ourselves is the most important thing we can do in this life. She writes that from the realm of death, she realized how powerful and special she was in the eyes of the Universe. Ultimately, she said, loving herself was what brought her back from the brink of death to where she is now.

All of this sounded lovely, but it didn't quite land for me until she made a really solid point. Namely, "the amount of love, respect, support and compassion I receive from others is in direct proportion to how much I love myself, because it's impossible to receive something unless I have a place to put it." And if that didn't bring it home, she pointed out that loving your neighbor *as thyself* doesn't work so well if you don't even love yourself.

If I wanted to love my neighbor as myself, I would have to love me first. Only then would I be replenished enough to be able to offer them anything. A dry well can offer no sustenance. But if you tap into the wellspring of self-love, you will have a continuous source of metaphoric fresh, hydrating water to offer all those who visit.

Your Greatest Form of Activism

I've become passionate about self-care as being the greatest form of activism available to women today.
DR. KELLY BROGAN, *Sounds True Self-Acceptance Summit*

Anita's Moorjani's NDE story is not an anomaly. Most NDE survivors, regardless of religion or lack thereof (including famous neurosurgeon, Dr. Eben Alexander), return from the other side with similar messages. Namely, we are dearly loved, we are never alone, and we are always safe. As I devoured NDE stories and heard these messages repeated over and over, my commitment to self-love was solidified. If the Universe loved me exactly as I was without condition, who was I not to embrace and love myself?

But what exactly does self-love look like in practice? Our culture often portrays self-loving care for women as a mani-pedi, a bubble bath, or a massage (all of which I myself enjoy and fully support). However, self-love goes beyond all that. It encompasses just about anything that directs kindness to yourself or that nourishes and replenishes you. This can include but is not limited to getting enough rest, eating healthy foods, meditating, practicing mindfulness, spending time in nature, participating in a hobby that brings you joy, spending quality time with friends and family, purchasing clothes that fit your body well and make you feel beautiful, or engaging in a spiritual practice that sustains you. Self-love even brings in lesser-known, more intangible components, such as drawing healthy boundaries and practicing self-compassion.

The Magical No

Disappoint everyone a little every day.
KELLY RIPA

Kimberley sat across from me looking completely drained. This wasn't surprising, as her doctor had recently told her she had adrenal fatigue. Quite a few of the women I coach have this issue. And for many of them, it stems from a similar problem: they don't know how to say no. They have kids, husbands, employers, PTAs, and various committees, all demanding the world of them. They have emptied their metaphoric cup one too many times without refilling from the wellspring of self-love and self-care. And they continue to say yes to everything, regardless of whether they have the time, energy, or desire to commit to these things.

Without proper boundaries around their time and energy, it is no wonder that they have reached the point of adrenal fatigue. You may think of boundaries as purely physical, like when someone awkwardly squishes up against you in a crowded subway, or a fellow guest at a dinner party is an annoyingly close-talker. But boundaries encompass so much more. And it is your right to set them wherever you are comfortable.

I love world-renowned shame researcher and *New York Times* bestselling author Brené Brown's practice around boundary setting on her time. When the head of the PTA invites her to say, make hundreds of cupcakes for the school fundraiser with little to no notice, she very calmly turns the ring on her finger three times to give herself a few moments to feel into the right answer. If it's not a full-body emphatic "Yes! I'd love to!" (read: it feels like freedom), she declines. Or at a bare minimum, she allows herself more time before committing to an answer. Her motto? Disappointment over resentment. In other words, she would rather disappoint the head of the PTA than fume with resentment at 3 a.m. as she labors over the cupcakes.

Practicing self-love means honoring your boundaries, just like Brené does. It is your right to say that magical word, "No." Remember that old phrase that "it's better to give than receive?"

It is *not* better to give than receive when you have nothing left to give. Heck, it's not even better to give than receive if you are merely depleted. Every time you turn down something that is not a clear yes, you keep your love cup above the minimum line. You have more energy and love to give to those people and activities you truly care about – the most important one being you!

Self-Compassion

> *Until you can extend that same grace and compassion and*
> *forgiveness to yourself that you want and claim ... you*
> *won't be able to actually have mercy for anybody else either*
> *because there will be this secret dark little part of you that*
> *looks up everyone else's failings and everyone else's errors*
> *and everyone else's shortcomings and says "they should've*
> *done better, they should've known better." And then we're just*
> *keeping everybody in Hell.*
>
> ELIZABETH GILBERT, *Sounds True Self-Acceptance Summit*

I am a big ol' cheerleader for self-love and self-care when it comes to my clients. I know this stuff works! One day, however, my dear client Caroline expressed some doubts. "If I'm always kind and loving to myself, and I turn down the volume on my task-master inner critic, how will I ever be productive or motivated to get anything done?" she asked. "Won't I just become a pile of lazy, self-loving mush?"

Fortunately, there is wonderful research on this very issue. Dr. Kristin Neff is an Associate Professor at the University of Texas at Austin and a pioneer in self-compassion research. She defines self-compassion as simply being a friend to yourself. But it's not just rainbows and unicorns – it has elements of support and protection, as well. Self-compassion can be fierce!

Her research has shown that self-compassion is actually linked to increased motivation. Self-compassionate people aim high and are less afraid to fail, thereby making them more inclined to try again and keep trying till they reach their goals. And lest you think self-compassionate people are more likely to let themselves off the hook when faced with taking personal responsibility, they are actually more likely to repair past harms. When it's internally safe to admit you are wrong and cut yourself some slack, apologies can be generously offered.

Bottom line, thanks to the pioneering research of Dr. Neff and others, the benefits of self-compassion (from increased motivation to improved health) are well-documented. And the good news is that practicing self-compassion is incredibly simple (although not always easy). Start by simply monitoring your self-talk. Is it critical? If so, ask yourself whether you would say this very same thing to your child or a dear friend you care about. My hunch is you wouldn't. Nip that self-criticism in the bud. Change the content of your self-talk. Say only those things that feel like freedom; eliminate any verbiage that makes you feel constricted and heavy inside.

And if you want to ramp it up a notch? Speak to yourself in a soft, soothing tone, like you would with a scared or hurt child. You can even hold your own hand or stroke your own arm gently. Yep, there's research behind these practices – a soothing voice and a soft touch, even if they're your own, are incredibly beneficial.

Your Most Important Marital Relationship

You might be wondering how we could come to the end of a chapter in a book written for unhappy wives without much mention of marriage. Simple – from my perspective, the most important relationship that you will ever enter into is with yourself. Self-love is an integral part of that relationship. It is a structural component of your very being, and your marriage is merely layered over the relationship with self. Put another way, relationship with self (including self-love) is the foundation; your marriage is a structure built on top.

And those vows you took at your wedding – probably some variation of loving and honoring your beloved? I invite you to make those vows to yourself. If you want gold stars, craft some new vows – from you to you. Remember the excitement of that heartfelt commitment, the shimmer of possibility and the future on the horizon? Create that for yourself and commit fully, till death do you part. For extra credit, see if you can let go of any worn-out stories that no longer fit – religious, cultural, or family stories that said you are flawed, unworthy, and come last. Now what if you knew that you were born magnificent, born worthy, born lovable, and born cherished by a benevolent Universe? What if you fully owned your value to the world? Craft your vows with this in mind. Record them in your journal and return to them when you need to be reminded of your most significant relationship.

Marry yourself first. Commit to loving and honoring yourself first. It is one of the least selfish actions you can take. And by getting in right relationship with yourself, you will greatly improve your chances of being in right relationship with others – your relationship with your spouse, whether you stay or go, is no exception.

CHAPTER 8

Future Tripping in a Good Way

You must give up the life you planned in order to embrace the
life that is waiting for you.

JOSEPH CAMPBELL

Wendy was one of my first clients. Soft-spoken and extremely creative, she was a gifted artist and a loving mother. She was also just about ready to leave her marriage. In our sessions, we worked through some of her marital resentments, we talked about some of her biggest fears around leaving, and my favorite part, we created a vision for what her future would look like on the other side of it all.

But we didn't create just any ordinary wish list. Instead, I led Wendy through a guided visualization designed to tap into the limitless possibilities in her creative right brain and the biggest vision of her Wise Authentic Self. As I walked Wendy through a day in her future new life, she described everything as it appeared to her, from the flooring in her new loft, to the forest trails she would run on afternoon breaks from painting, to the warm campfire she would sit by as her evening drew to a close.

Wendy did end up leaving her marriage, a decision she weighed for quite some time. I continued to work with her as she navigated the legal process and stepped into a new life as a single woman. We returned to her vision periodically, especially in times when things got hard, as they often inevitably do at various points during any divorce, no matter how amicable. She remembered and drew comfort from the way she envisioned she would feel at a time not too far off in the future: easeful, loving, and inspired. She did her best to bring these feeling states into the present so that she would attract more of the same into her current life. She did the work and she kept moving forward. It paid off.

Several months went by, and I didn't see Wendy. When she returned for a session, she was bursting to share some exciting updates. Previously, she had some concerns about where she would move when she left her marital home. She was excited to report that she'd found a perfect cozy loft in a beautiful part of town. And the apartment she described matched almost identically the loft she'd seen in her vision months prior!

Mapping Your Future

Wendy's story of a future life vision manifesting in physical reality might seem a bit miraculous. But it's not uncommon. I have now lost count of the stories I've heard from mentors, friends, colleagues, and clients alike about images from vision boards and exercises like that described above becoming real – down to the tiniest details.

During that time when your marriage is on the precipice, it can often be a welcome respite to let your mind wander, let your imagination play, and see if your Wise Authentic Self has some ideas of what a new life might look like. It's like future tripping (i.e., worrying about the future), but with a positive spin.

I still have a page torn from one of my all-time favorite books I read over and over during my divorce, Martha Beck's *Steering by Starlight*. By following Martha's prompts, I created a map of what I wanted my life to look like someday. I imagined what I would be, do, and have; who I would love; and by whom I would be loved. During my separation, and then later during my divorce proceedings, I returned to this page like a kid returning to wrapped presents under a Christmas tree. I wasn't exactly sure what was in store, but the anticipation of something good around the corner gave me the hope and strength to move forward when the going got tough.

I'll provide some suggested exercises at the end of this chapter to help bring your vision out of the ethers. But first, I'd like to give you some reassurance that it's certainly not mandatory to know exactly what your future will look. Unless you are Nostradamus, that's darn near impossible anyway. I myself had little more than an amorphous idea of what I wanted my life to look like after my divorce, much less what I could definitively predict. In my experience, however, meandering on your journey allows room for a little magic. And taking risks makes the most gratifying rewards possible. Just ask the Polynesians.

A Two-Thousand Mile Canoe Trip to Your Destiny

The Polynesians were the original inhabitants of a little island chain you might have heard of called Hawaii. At first blush, this may not sound so dramatic. However, let me tell you this was no ordinary feat, as Hawaii is one of the most remote places on earth. The time was around 300-600 A.D., and the Polynesians were living on the Marquesas Islands, which are located over 2,000 miles from the Hawaiian Islands.

To get there, the Polynesians had no fancy equipment or maps to chart their course. Instead, they used a method of navigation called "wayfinding," which relies solely on natural signs such as the direction of the waves, the position of certain stars, and the formation of clouds (combined with a healthy dose of human intuition). Their primary voyaging craft was simply a double canoe made of two hulls connected by lashed crossbeams.

Oh, and one more teensy detail: When they set sail, the Polynesians did not actually have solid proof that the Hawaiian Islands even existed – just a hunch, based on watching certain bird species migrate to and from the islands the Polynesians called home. To sum it all up, the Polynesians basically found a little needle of an island chain in a vast 10-million square mile haystack of sea. And they weren't sure that little needle was even there when they left the comfort of their home.

Although various theories have been thrown about to explain why on earth the Polynesians would have undertaken such a journey, I agree with those who say it was motivated by a spirit of adventure inherent to their culture. They had a desire for growth, for expansion, and for finding something more. Metaphorically, I related to this desire in my own life. Perhaps you do, too.

There I was, living on a gorgeous island I called my life. I could easily have stayed and enjoyed its pleasures, focusing on the sheer beauty and ease of it all while simultaneously overlooking the ugly parts (i.e., my tumultuous and lonely marriage). At a certain point, I could no longer ignore the call to more, and while I was likely way less equipped for such a journey than the Polynesians, I set sail from my old life.

Now maybe you don't want to match the crazy, courageous seafaring ways of the Polynesians, and that's okay. Chances are, following your "something more" will not entail risking your life. But risk can be relative, and following your heart and spirit in your relationship may feel pretty damn scary. In those moments, just call upon that same wayfinding spirit of those islanders, and channel your inner Polynesian to navigate toward what beckons you from the horizon.

Just imagine how marvelous it must have felt for those travelers, after a month or more at sea, to finally spot the land they intuitively knew would be waiting for them. And now imagine in your own life how incredible it could feel to set foot on your very own Hawaii (metaphorically ... or maybe not!). I encourage you to carry this vision with you when you ready your boat and set sail for the *something more* you know is waiting for you.

Don't Worry About the Cursed Hows – Just Look for the Breadcrumbs

I left my marriage being certain of little save for what freedom felt like (see Chapter 4). So I followed that. But that sense of freedom didn't come with a map of where I was headed. For a Type A former lawyer like me, this plan (or lack thereof) was terrifying. What I have come to understand in the years since, however, is that all I had to do was steer myself in the general direction of my dreams, and the Universe would help me fill in the remaining details.

At the time, my "dream" consisted of a strong urge to return to the West Coast full-time and the desire to be of service to others. That's about the extent of it. So when Washington felt more like freedom than California, I moved to Seattle. And when life coach training felt more like freedom than taking the Washington Bar Exam, I signed up.

Over time, my dream began to take more shape. I envisioned creating a coaching practice, a radio show, and buying a house in my new favorite city (Seattle, of course!). I even came up with some bigger goals around income, ideal clients, writing a book, and reaching large numbers of people with an inspiring and meaningful message. Yet I still had no idea *how* all of this was going to happen.

But here's the thing I learned from *New York Times* bestselling author and motivational speaker, Mike Dooley: It is not our job to worry about "the cursed hows." I wouldn't have believed this had someone told me back then. In my old life, I grabbed onto goals with the white-knuckled death grip of a passenger on the world's tallest roller coaster. I would have driven myself crazy with worry and anxiety over how everything was going to come together and why it wasn't happening faster.

But I've now witnessed enough validation in my own life, as well as the lives of my mentors and clients, to know the profound truth of Johann Wolfgang von Goethe's famous quote that "at the moment of commitment the entire universe conspires to assist you." It really doesn't matter whether you believe this assistance is coming from Source, God, Love with a capital "L," the grand burrito in the sky, or simply the intelligence of life that heals our cuts and signals the birds to go south in winter. Provided that you're willing to be just a tiny bit open, like those southbound birds, you will be guided.

In my own life, with each step forward, all I did was regularly reassess whether I still felt free. And as I simply continued moving toward freedom, lo and behold, breadcrumbs would appear for me to follow ... like meeting a kind and amazing man in the most serendipitous of ways with whom I fell arse-over-teakettle in love, right around the time my failing marriage gasped its last dying breath. Just when I was ready to pack a moving truck for my return to the West Coast after my marriage ended, this man invited me to move to his hometown of Seattle in a little corner of the Pacific Northwest ... and although I'd never been north of San Francisco, I accepted.

Shortly after our move, we discussed a mutual desire for an international adventure that simply had to involve elephants and Thailand. Soon thereafter, we received a flyer in the mailbox of our rental bungalow in Capitol Hill for a course offered at a nearby community college on how to volunteer abroad. The photo on the front? The course's instructor smiling broadly next to an enormous elephant in a beautiful rain forest. In Thailand. We signed up immediately.

After completing that course, we set off for a volunteer adventure that would take us from Spain, through Russia and Mongolia, on to China, then Thailand. As our journey abroad drew to a close in Indonesia, anxiety crept in. What would I do when I returned to "real life"? Although I received a divorce settlement that bought me a couple years of time to find new and meaningful work, I still had no idea what that would be.

Then, during a stopover in Bali where I had good Internet access for the first time in over a month, I decided to tackle my overflowing email inbox. The first message I landed on was an invitation to join Martha Beck's next life coach training program, which synchronistically started the month we were to return to the United States.

I'd attended one of Martha's workshops in her hometown of San Luis Obispo shortly before heading out on our international adventures. It was life-changing. So I thought, "What the heck? Maybe life coach training would be a nine-month version of that four-day workshop." Unlike my painstaking decisions on 1) whether go to law school; and then 2) which school to attend, this was a no-brainer. Quite literally. It was a decision made straight from my heart to the "Register Now!" button on Martha's website. No thought, just following freedom.

Lo and behold, I liked coaching ("Duh!" said my Wise Authentic Self with a knowing smile). And through that life coach training program, my radio show and new coaching practice began to take shape, as did the desire to help others through the Hell-and-back path I'd already traveled, from the painful decision to leave my marriage through to divorce.

All the pro-and-con lists and rational thinking in the world could never have taken me on such a wild and wonderful adventure to where I sit writing this book. It was only by following the breadcrumbs that appeared before me and trusting that more would appear that I have this story to tell and this healing to share.

Our job is not to figure out the cursed hows. Frankly, even if I'd known the path, the effortful approach I likely would have taken would have involved much more struggle than the way things actually unfolded. Instead, the events in my life took form with ease and seeming magic as I waited patiently (alright, not so patiently sometimes) for my next breadcrumb. That is not to say there was no fear or hard work. Certain events over the past few years have challenged me greatly! And still ... I have not been disappointed yet. In fact, those breadcrumbs have become more like toast points these days – you can't miss 'em!

Your High End Goals

In Collaborative Family Law (which we'll discuss in greater detail in Chapter 12 on Graceful Divorce), the parties agree to settle their dispute outside of a courtroom. The process is gentler than the traditional family law model, offering much more emotional support with a focus on problem solving rather than fighting to win. My husband and I chose to go the collaborative route in our divorce.

At the beginning of the collaborative process in certain states, the parties come up with "High End Goals." Such goals are designed to identify what matters most to them, how they want to conduct themselves, and how they want their life to be. Examples might include communicating with kindness or ensuring that the kids don't become pawns in the process. When tensions rise or the parties reach an impasse, they can return to these goals to ground themselves, realign to their values, and continue forward with more positivity and composure.

Regardless of whether you get divorced, setting some High End Goals for yourself can provide a foundation for you to return to if you lose your way in deciding how to proceed in your marriage. These particular goals are not meant to be a wish list for material possessions or position statements on what you believe you need (e.g., "I must get the house" or "I need a guaranteed settlement of X amount to survive"). There is certainly nothing wrong with such lists – I made them myself when the time came. The focus of this exercise, however, is more along the lines of a list of non-negotiables for your life and heart. These are closely-held values. They should feel like freedom. And they come from your Wise Authentic Self.

Your goals might include items like "I will speak my truth honestly yet constructively" or "I will trust my gut when making big decisions" or "I will act from a place of love, even if I want to strangle my husband." Now is your chance. Using your trusty journal, identify five High End Goals that will frame any decisions you will make or actions you will take around your marriage.

Now that you've started moving in the general direction of your dreams, you're following the breadcrumbs, and you've set your High End Goals for framing your path forward, it's time to start visioning!

Visualization Works

It is no secret that many professional athletes use visualization to achieve desired outcomes in their respective sports. As long ago as the 1960s, tennis star Billie Jean King was incorporating the practice of using highly detailed mental images to increase her chances of success. Golf legend Jack Nicklaus and America's gymnastic sweetheart and Olympic gold medalist Mary Lou Retton credit their athletic triumphs to visualization. These days, the techniques are getting even more sophisticated, and incorporate the senses in addition to mental images. Take US freestyle aerials Olympian, Emily Cook, who says, "You have to smell it. You have to hear it. You have to feel it, everything."

There is also quite a bit of research on the subject, lending credibility to this practice. For example, various studies have divided participants into groups and monitored improvement in throwing darts, making basketball free throws, or other athletic endeavors using some combination of physical practice and visualization. Time after time, those participants using visualization alone or in conjunction with physical practice improved their scores approximately as much as those who engaged in actual physical practice, and at times even surpassed it.

In just one example, a 2013 study from the University of Texas had participating students merely visualize lifting a dumbbell with their right arm over the course of six weeks. At the end of the study, those students were 11 percent stronger in their right arm – and they never even lifted an actual weight!

I share this research to highlight the fact that visualization works. But you don't have to be an elite athlete to incorporate it into your life, or use it only in a sports setting. Visualizing your ideal life is a powerful tool for moving in the direction of your best destiny. While the High End Goals you identified above are an anchor for your deeply-held values and the foundation from which your action will flow, the exercises below are designed to assist you in forming a vision for what you want to create in your life as you move forward.

Suggested Visualization and Manifestation Practices

If you've read *The Secret*, you may have heard of a manifestation tool called a vision board. The practice consists of selecting images from magazines, books, or the trusty ol' Interwebs that depict people, places, and things that you want, that light you up, and that portray the way you want to feel or live. If you've spent any time in coach-y, metaphysical circles, you know that parties where you create a vision board abound.

I'll be really honest, vision boarding ain't my jam. I've attended these parties, I've made vision boards on my own, and I just don't particularly enjoy the practice. If you, like me, don't care for this activity, this does not mean you are doomed to a dim, boring future. Far from it! The good news is that your entire life is a prayer – a beautiful, living prayer that changes over time as desires and dreams arise and are fulfilled, and new ones are added. Even if you don't hand over a detailed list or picture to the Universe, your Wise Authentic Self knows the desires and dreams that will be most meaningful to your soul and the inmost parts of you.

But it's still incredibly powerful and fun to do a little dreaming. Below I have included some of my favorite manifesting tools curated from a variety of sources. You don't have to use all of them (unless you feel drawn to them all). Simply select one or two that resonate for you and incorporate them into a daily or weekly practice. Treat them like brushing your teeth. In other words, it's great if you are regular and consistent in your practice, but it won't kill you to miss it every now and then.

Creative Workshopping – This process is based on the teachings of Abraham Hicks. Identify and write down in your journal various things you want in the big areas of your life, such as your work, your body and health, and your relationships. You might say, "I'd like my body to be stronger," or "I want to love what I do for my career." Now, below each of your desire statements, write several reasons *why* you want these particular things. For example, below "I'd like my body to be stronger," you might say "...because I can do more outdoor activities that I enjoy" and "...because I can play sports with my kids." Or below the statement, "I want to love what I do for my career," you might write "...because meaningful work is important to me" and "...because I want to look forward to Mondays for a change."

This particular exercise is a great way of not only identifying your desires, but also focusing your energy around them, as well as lessening resistance and increasing motivation to bring these desires to fruition.

Treasuring – This process comes from Martha Beck. For this exercise, close your eyes and allow yourself to envision in your mind's eye the things you most desire, such as the business you want to start or the book you want to write. Remember US freestyle aerials Olympian Emily Cook, from earlier in this chapter, who said when it comes to visualization, "You have to feel it"? When you are doing your treasuring, instead of merely imagining a 2D image, really drop into it with all five senses. For example, envision holding your finished book in your hands. Feel its hardbound cover, see the picture on the front, smell the new paper as you flip through the pages, and hear the compliments you will receive when your friends and family read it. For those things you truly want, regularly spend several minutes visualizing them in your mind's eye while using all five of your senses.

God Box – Place a box of your choice in a prominent place in your home, such as the table in your entryway or on your kitchen counter. The box can be simple or ornate; you can decorate it or leave it as-is. It should be around the size of a shoebox or a little larger. The idea is to place in the box things you come across during your day-to-day life that are meaningful to you, make you happy, or light you up. You might put in the box a four-leaf clover you found on a walk, a ticket stub from a super-fun concert, or a card you received from a friend. It can also contain images from magazines or newspapers that move you or capture a feeling you want to embody. The God Box is similar to a vision board, but it allows for 3D objects and accumulation of more items. After a month or so, go through your God Box and see if you notice any themes amongst its contents, such as a large number of nature-based items, like rocks, flowers, and leaves. Notice if there are any surprises. What do the Box's contents suggest about your dreams and desires? Not only will this Box serve as a container for meaningful moments in your life, it also can provide clues as to where your Wise Authentic Self most wants to lead you.

Photo Album – This process is adapted from Mike Dooley. Create a photo album portraying the life you wish to have. Print out images from the Internet or cut images from magazines and newspapers. Place them in the album and write descriptions of each scene. You can also superimpose or Photoshop yourself into these images. For example, you might include a photo of a beautiful beach in Bali, and place a photo of yourself in the scene with a description like, "Me in Bali enjoying my month-long vacation." Or next to a photo from the stage at a TED event in a major city, "The view from the stage where I gave my first TED Talk for an audience of 1,000 people." Include as many pages and as many scenes as you want in this album, writing the descriptions as if the events depicted are a done deal and have already happened in your life.

Mantras – There are a myriad of authors, spiritual teachers, coaches, and healers who encourage using mantras.

A mantra is simply a sound or idea used as a focal point, usually during meditation. It is a way of bringing yourself back to home base, or to the present moment. Although there are an endless number of mantras one can use or create, I personally love the Ultimate Success Mantra developed by Dr. Gay Hendricks. For over 30 years, Dr. Hendricks has helped clients, from small business owners to celebrities and CEOs of Fortune 100 companies, overcome barriers to happiness and fulfillment. In his *New York Times* bestseller, *The Big Leap*, Dr. Hendricks explains his Ultimate Success Mantra as "a set of instructions to your conscious and unconscious mind, designed to inform all your actions and decisions." He goes on to explain that over time, your life will conform to the intention contained in the mantra, which goes: *I expand in abundance, success, and love every day, as I inspire those around me to do the same.* I love this simple yet powerful mantra, and use it almost daily. Feel free to adopt this Ultimate Success Mantra, or select another of your own choosing or creation. It is key to ensure your mantra is written in present tense (i.e., "I expand in abundance" not "I *will* expand in abundance"), and that it conveys a positive intention about some area(s) of your being or life.

Your Wise Authentic Self Knows Best

A quick note about the tools and exercises above. They are wonderful ways to dream and scheme about the life you most want to have. And like my client Wendy discovered, they can provide inspiring material to return to, especially when it's difficult to see the light at the end of the tunnel when your marriage is draining you or divorce proceedings are weighing you down. I myself use many of these exercises on a consistent basis to this day, around my relationships and my work.

With each of them, however, the idea is to release your white-knuckled death grip on a particular outcome. That kind of grasping tends to pinch you off from the flow of universal energy. They also are not a guarantee of an outcome. After *The Secret* made its big splash, many an eager manifestor quickly realized that merely visualizing that Mercedes did not mean the abundance would magically arrive to support such a purchase. And that actually may be a good thing.

You may remember my dear Small Self, Holly. She was quite convinced that all we needed for total and complete happiness in this lifetime was a killer bod, a fancy graduate education, and a fat bank account. Like a kid who thinks the latest video game or prettiest new Barbie will complete their life, I discovered, these things were nice, but ultimately they didn't fulfill me. And like a patient parent who knows that a kid's best interest is served through love and unconditional presence, not stuff, your Wise Authentic Self ultimately knows what will best serve you.

We come here for so much more than the accumulation of material goods or shallow interests. That's why the Law of Attraction is not the whole story. For every person who didn't manifest that Mercedes by merely visualizing it, there is a Wise Authentic Self that knows there is a bigger plan that may provide way more meaning and growth than a luxury automobile – or who knows, maybe the Mercedes didn't arrive because there's a Ferrari in your future instead.

All that to say, use the tools above to create a general vision of your best life, but always leave room for your Wise Authentic Self to lovingly step in and direct you to the people, places, and things that will be the most fulfilling to your heart and soul.

CHAPTER 9

Getting Shamelessly Spiritual

We are not human beings having a spiritual experience.
We are spiritual beings having a human experience.
PIERRE TEILHARD DE CHARDIN

When I first met my client Milly, I liked her immediately. No-nonsense with a charming personality and a wicked sense of humor, she was ready to roll up her sleeves and get to work. She was already divorced, but acknowledged she still had some healing to do. Her anger at her ex-husband hadn't fully diminished, and she was concerned her kids were bearing the brunt of her frustrations.

As is customary with all my clients, I asked Milly a series of intake questions at the beginning of our engagement in order to get to know her a bit better. One of my typical questions is whether a client has a spiritual or religious practice. Milly had no such practice, so I made a mental note to not be too heavy handed when it came to the spiritual stuff.

One day, as we worked the steps of my program together, Milly mentioned that she'd created a list after her divorce, along the lines of the statements you might come up with using the Creative Workshopping exercise found in Chapter 8. On her list, she had identified five or six things she wanted to experience or accomplish in the year following her divorce. It included items like finding a new job and meeting a new love interest. Although it had not yet been a year since her divorce, she was excited that almost all of the items listed had come to fruition.

According to Milly, once she identified a want or need, it was as if unseen forces were moving behind the scenes to accommodate her request. Her new job, for example, had come about in the most serendipitous of circumstances, and was a perfect fit in terms of company culture and salary. I invited Milly to add to her list as she began to cross items off and really pay attention to how these things began to manifest in her life, to make note of how things began to appear in seemingly miraculous ways. Perhaps she was more than a mere meat suit over bones. Perhaps she was connected to something larger that always had her back. Much like Milly, I, too, was initially hesitant to believe that the Universe might be conspiring to assist in my own life. That all changed, however, with the number 11.

Getting Inked by the Universe

Growing up, anytime my friends and I happened to catch the clock as it struck 11:11, we'd squeal, "11:11! Make a wish!" And we would. By the time I hit adulthood, I was over those silly superstitions, though. Still immersed in my own study of religious history, I also remained skeptical of most organized religions. I hadn't yet found my footing in my faith in a higher power. As a result, I didn't pray much at that time, either.

But then came a time when I was so torn between a marriage I knew I needed to leave and a life I was too afraid to leave behind, that I felt as if I would be rent in two. What I was doing was clearly not working. I was desperate for help, and I really didn't care where it came from. I was willing to try just about anything. Around that time, I came across a quote often attributed to Albert Einstein that says, "The most important decision we make is whether we believe we live in a friendly or hostile universe." I didn't know why, but this quote resonated profoundly for me. I decided to pretend as if it were a friendly Universe – a fake-it-'til-I-make-it approach to my faith. And I was not disappointed.

Around that same time, I began to see 11:11 on the clock religiously (pun intended). Every twelve hours, it felt like those numbers locked onto my brain and drew my startled attention to the clock. Making a wish on those special numbers felt good. It became reassuring. In my own individual way, I was beginning to pray.

My prayer at every 11:11 was simple. I wished that whatever was supposed to happen would happen, whatever that was. And I asked for peace, something that we'd never had much of around my home. This was a marked departure from my usual MO of diligently working to force a perfect life into place. But all of this had felt like a lifelong exercise of trying to fit a giant square peg into a tiny round hole. It never occurred to me to see whether there might be a perfectly shaped square hole waiting for my square peg. Through my last-ditch prayer effort, though, I found it.

I didn't realize it at the time, but by turning over the reins to unseen forces because I was simply too tired to carry them anymore, and by asking for whatever was supposed to happen, it was like sending an emergency flare up to the cosmos. To my amazement, help began to arrive and the breadcrumbs I mentioned earlier began to appear.

Among so many other serendipitous gifts and events, the peace I'd been asking for arrived in the form of the dear safe man I fell in love with as my marriage drew to a close. He radiated peace, something I'd never experienced with my husband. Turns out he had a little affinity for 11:11, too. As we left the country for our international volunteer adventure, we noticed our flight number was 1111. The "God winks" continued to follow us, showing up everywhere, as 11 continued to appear in hotel room numbers, license plates, and other seemingly random places around the world.

I had given up (at least for the time being) my years-in-advance Type A planning, my grasping attachment to certain outcomes, and my wrestling of square pegs into round holes. I was living moment-to-moment and trusting that it would all work out as it was supposed to. In the beginning, I was able to relinquish control due to sheer exhaustion with hands thrown up in frustration; soon, my exhaustion turned to trust. That trust only strengthened, when gift after serendipitous gift continued to appear. Like the near-death experience survivors in Chapter 7, I was beginning to believe I was dearly loved and never alone.

With time, my desire to connect with this benevolent Universe I perceived around me began to grow. I discovered spiritual bookstores that housed beautiful texts from many wisdom traditions. Teachers met me on my path to show me that there were many ways to connect to a power greater than myself. They reminded me that I was a magnificent spiritual being with a purpose, not merely a flawed, powerless human.

Outside the bounds of dogma, I began to develop my own relationship with Jesus and other ascended masters like Buddha, Thoth, Melchizedek, and Quan Yin. I absorbed all of this like a dried-up sponge, and it fed me in a way nothing ever had. In gratitude, I ultimately tattooed 11:11 on the back of my neck. I never wanted to forget the goodness I experienced when I asked my Wise Authentic Self and the Universe to take the lead.

Much-Needed Perspective

It's possible you might be backing away from this book slowly after I started talking metaphysical bookstores and ascended masters. If so, don't worry – I promise to keep the woo woo to a minimum for the rest of this chapter! It also is not my intent to strong-arm you into a spiritual practice. After my own religious wounding, it took me many years to come back around to the idea of a God in any form. Whether you are an atheist or a religious fundamentalist, you are welcome here.

I bring all of this up primarily for one reason: Perspective. Before my 11:11 conversion experience, I was myopically focused on my marriage and my life. Not only did it feel like the decision around my marriage was life and death, but I felt like I was all alone in making it. The weight of the world was on my shoulders, and one wrong move would ruin my life. But that's the thing about perspective. It gives you ... perspective. With a wider lens, I could now see the forest, not just the immediate trees in front of me.

That's what spirituality does – it places you in a bigger picture with greater meaning. But don't take my word for it.

Famed shame researcher Brené Brown has done some wonderful research on resiliency, or the ability to overcome adversity and stressful situations. One of the key elements that she's found in building resiliency is spirituality. By spirituality she isn't necessarily talking about religion, but instead "the belief in connection, a power greater than self, and interconnections grounded in love and compassion."

I tend to take the Alcoholics Anonymous approach to the whole higher power business. As it says in the Big Book, each person should choose a God of his or her own understanding. That God can look like the intelligence of the Universe that heals your cuts without you doing a thing, a divine universal creator, or a simple belief in the power of connection with others when spending time in a group. The recognition of a benevolent power greater than self may just give you the support and empowerment you need to make the tough decisions about your marriage that previously felt too big, too scary to handle on your own.

Get Shamelessly Spiritual

Like me, you may have received a healthy dose of Emily Post's etiquette growing up. If so, topics like money, politics, and religion were not to be discussed in polite company. I'm tired of limiting myself to superficial small talk, though. I want the interconnections Brené Brown spoke of, those "grounded in love and compassion" and those filled with meaning. So let's get a little shamelessly spiritual!

Don't worry – you don't have to go to church for this one (unless you want to). All it involves is establishing a daily practice. By daily practice, I'm referring to something you do on a regular basis (ideally daily) that allows you to connect with your Wise Authentic Self and the higher power of your understanding. You can write in a journal, meditate, read from one of your favorite wisdom texts, or simply sit quietly in your favorite spot in nature. What you do is less important than your intent behind it and your simple willingness to show up for yourself. By creating a container of space and time, you allow connection to the greatest wisdom your highest self has to offer.

When your Small Self is overwhelmed with fear and unable to make a decision around your marriage, you can return to the foundation of your daily practice for accessing guidance. Over time you may, like me, discover that you are infinitely supported by a friendly Universe. And from that vantage point, you are a heckuva lot more empowered to make the right decision about your marriage – whatever that decision is.

The Muscle You Need to Start Working

Shortly before I got separated, I found a beautiful 8x10 lithograph that said "Trust Your Gut." That piece traveled with me and was prominently displayed in every tiny studio apartment I rented while I was going through my separation into my divorce. I knew instinctively that this little art piece would be a tangible reminder of my desire for congruency between my head, heart, and gut.

It's an oft-repeated cliché of a phrase, but I didn't really care. Later, it took on new meaning for me once I discovered the "gut brain," more technically known as the enteric nervous system. This intricate web of nerves lining our guts has been nicknamed by scientists as our "second brain." It contains about 100 million neurons, more than in either the spinal cord or the peripheral nervous system. Thus, the reason it's called a brain in its own right. Unlike the brain in your head, however, your gut brain has access to more than a pro and con list – it is an incredible source of intuitive information.

So is the brain in your heart. Yep, you heard that right – you have a little brain in your heart made of cells that think, feel, and remember independently of the brain. Thanks to the pioneering research of the HeartMath Institute, we now know the human heart is so much more than a biological organ for pumping blood – it also is an essential source of wisdom and intuition. There are 40,000 specialized neurons in there, forming a communication network right inside your heart. And through heart-brain coherence, we can intentionally access states of deep intuition (see www.heartmath.com for more information and a fantastic Quick Coherence Technique).

Keep in mind that human intuitive abilities come in many flavors, much like artistic abilities come in different forms. Just like certain people connect with artistic expression in an auditory way through music, others do better visually with oil painting, for example. Similarly, intuition is accessed and arrives in packaging that is unique to the receiver, as well. Intuition is also much like a muscle. In other words, we all have muscles, but you need to exercise them to not only get comfortable using them, but to strengthen them. Once you've got some intuitive muscle mass, you will find it is far easier to connect with your Wise Authentic Self.

To determine how you best connect with your intuition and strengthen it, I'd like to introduce you to the *clairs*. The clairs are the various ways in which humans receive intuitive information through the senses. See the list below for an explanation of each of them. Although you may find that you are strong in several of these areas, chances are one or two of these will be your dominant intuitive strength(s).

Clairvoyance = Clear Seeing & Vision

Those who are clairvoyant are highly visual people who typically notice how things look (e.g., the way someone is dressed, the design of a room, or the presentation of a meal) before they focus on anything else. They likely have an eye for detail and are visually creative. They are able to visualize people, places, and things in their mind's eye. For example, they can easily picture objects when they close their eyes (e.g., visualizing how a room will look with the addition of a new couch or how well a pair of shoes will match an outfit). Images of the past, present, and future flash through their mind, much like a daydream. They receive intuitive information through mental pictures or more visual stimuli.

Clairaudience = Clear Hearing

Those who are clairaudient are usually sensitive to noise. They receive intuitive information through words or sounds heard inside (or sometimes even outside) their mind. They may hear buzzing or experience ringing in their ears, or a voice may pop into their head, directing them to do something that turns out to be helpful. They also may hear music without a physical source or awaken with a song playing in their head.

Clairsentience = Clear Feeling & Sensing

Those who are clairsentient tend to interact with the world through their physical and emotional feelings. They often are accused of being "too sensitive." Sometimes, they may even confuse others' feelings for their own, as they may be highly empathic. They may make decisions based on how something or someone feels to them. They may recognize an intuitive hit through a particular physical or emotional sensation (e.g., getting the chills upon hearing a piece of accurate or significant information, or suddenly becoming very weary in the presence of someone they do not like).

Claircognizance = Clear Knowing

Those who are claircognizant tend to be analytical and intellectual. They know things without necessarily being able to explain how or why. Such knowledge may simply pop into their head, seemingly out of nowhere. Often, they assume the information they receive is common knowledge, but usually it is not. Claircognizance is my primary intuitive strength. I will never forget seeing two friends at a party, both of whom were married to other people at the time. Although they were not particularly flirty or doing anything remotely inappropriate, I suddenly *knew* they were having an affair. About a year later, my suspicion was confirmed when one of their spouses discovered some incriminating evidence. This particular clair is one of the tougher intuitive strengths to identify, as it does not come with tangible signs, like receiving a mental image (clairvoyance) or hearing a voice (clairaudience). Claircognizant individuals must simply have faith in their inner knowing. Over time, hopefully they will receive enough validation of their hunches to continue trusting them.

Clairalience = Clear Smelling

Those who are clairalient have the ability to detect smells that have no apparent physical source. In her book *Surviving Death: A Journalist Investigates Evidence for an Afterlife,* New York *Times* bestselling author Leslie Kean writes about a case where, following the death of an avid cigar smoker, a couple of his close friends smelled strong cigar smoke in a new car, as well as the cockpit of a plane. Both the car and plane were previously smoke-free areas, yet they were able to pick up the strong odor of cigar smoke. Other examples might include smelling a deceased relative's favorite perfume when no one else is around, or picking up the scent of a particularly meaningful flower with no plants in sight.

Clairgustance = Clear Tasting

Those who are clairgustant often have a heightened sense of taste. Similar to clairalients who are able to *smell* something without a physical source, these individuals are able to *taste* something without an apparent source. For example, someone who is clairgustant might taste the distinctive caramel flavor of their deceased grandfather's favorite Werther's Original hard candy without any sweets in the vicinity.

After reading the above descriptions, you may have a pretty good idea of your strongest intuitive ability. Another way to figure this out is to simply sit quietly wherever you are, and notice your surroundings. Really take it all in. Now, close your eyes, breathe deeply, and recall what caught your attention as you processed the environment around you. Do you have a *feeling* (physical or emotional) about it? Is it the *sight* of the scenery and the colors that stands out? Do you *hear, smell,* or *taste* something as you mentally revisit your surroundings? Or perhaps you simply have a *knowing* about it all?

No matter how the information arrives, it is essential to remember that your intuitive guidance is always benevolent – it will never tell you to harm yourself or another! If you'd still like a little more assistance in determining your intuitive strengths, there are plenty of fun online quizzes you can take to help you figure it out. Once you know which intuitive ability or abilities you favor, you can start strengthening this muscle through practice and begin receiving all the amazing guidance your Wise Authentic Self has to offer.

You Do You

Having perspective while making a decision as critical as whether or not to leave a marriage is absolutely necessary. A spiritual practice of some sort is one of the best ways to gain that perspective. But vibrant spirituality does not require membership with a certain religion or adherence to any certain creed. There are so many paths for exploring magic, mystery, and the Divine, and there are so many ways to access the wisdom that comes from your Wise Authentic Self and the higher power of your understanding.

You can take a gentle approach, as my client Milly did, and simply begin by experimenting with the Universe. Playfully put forth requests or desires and see what comes back, feeling for guidance from unseen forces as the Universe conspires to assist you. Or you can, as I did, take a more cannonball approach, jumping in with a splash by heading straight to the nearest metaphysical bookstore, followed by tattooing auspicious numbers on your neck.

Either way, this book provides my own anecdotal experiences, a few suggestions for establishing a spiritual practice, and recommendations for using your own distinctive spirituality for peace and guidance in your life. I encourage you to explore what works best for you. What feels like freedom? And what lights up your Wise Authentic Self? Like exercise, it is important to find the activities you actually enjoy, the ones that invigorate you and leave you feeling healthier and stronger.

Once you know what works for you, make it a part of your daily life, weaving this perspective and wisdom into all areas. When it comes time for tough decisions about your marriage, you will feel less alone and more equipped to make the right decision.

CHAPTER 10

Radical Honesty

The truth will set you free... but first it will piss you off.
GLORIA STEINEM

You Gotta Move the Leaves

Pretend with me, if you will, that you are walking in the woods on a lovely day in October. Fallen leaves cover the ground in a beautiful display of reds, yellows, oranges, and browns. All of a sudden, a large dog jumps out from behind a tree and bares its teeth at you menacingly as it snarls and growls. You immediately go into fight, flight, or freeze mode. You might even have a defensive, angry response toward the dog's aggression, something along the lines of, "Oh heck no, you are *not* going to hurt me today!" Just then, a small gust of wind rustles the leaves, moving them to reveal that the dog's leg is actually caught in a trap. You quickly realize the dog's aggressive reaction is due to its terror and severe pain. Immediately, you are moved into a state of compassion.

The purpose of this chapter is to help you remove any metaphoric leaves that may be obstructing your view of your spouse and your marriage. With a clear, honest look at what's really happening, including any painful traps around your beloved's leg, you may have more compassion as you evaluate how you'd like to proceed in your relationship.

Over the course of the next few pages, I am going to ask you to take a really honest look at yourself in the mirror, and a really intense look at your marriage. At times, this chapter may seem harsh. But if you've stuck with me this far, I know you can handle it. You probably would not still be reading if you didn't want to do the work. You might even get angry with me. That's okay, too. In fact, I expect all of these things, just as I anticipate such reactions when I work with my clients on getting radically honest about their marriages, the patterns they helped create, the wounds they may have inflicted, and the part they played in things getting to the point they are. All I ask is that you approach this work with openness, curiosity, and integrity.

And a quick disclaimer before we dive in: If you've been married to an abuser, an addict, a narcissist, a sociopath, or a psychopath, I want you to be extra-gentle with yourself here. If your spouse falls into any of the above categories, chances are much of the conflict, gaslighting, and crazy-making going on in your relationship were not your doing. I do not want you to use this work to further wound or punish yourself.

The truth is always kind, and it will set you free ... but it might just piss you off first. Ready?

The Dirty Ugly

When Marjorie first sat down in my office, she was seething with anger and resentment at her husband. She easily rattled off a list of all the things that were wrong with him, followed by all the wrongs he had committed against her. She said things like, "He's so selfish," "He expects me to do everything," and "He's just so unkind." I didn't doubt the veracity of her statements, and I certainly didn't doubt the feelings and emotions that were coming up for her. Holding space for a client to share such hurts is part of my job. And for the client, sharing these wounds for the first time with at least one compassionate witness is often the initial step of the healing process.

Over time, as we progressed in our work together, she was ready for some advanced maneuvers (as you now are, too). I gave Marjorie a homework assignment I'm now going to give to you. I'd like you to write to your spouse what I call a "Dirty Ugly Letter." Your spouse will never read this letter – it is for your eyes and purposes only. In it, I want you to articulate all the things you are angry about or all the ways you have been hurt or wronged by this person. You can even tell them how they should act or what they should do about their wrongs.

I call it the Dirty Ugly Letter because I want it to be as angry and bratty as possible. I want it to be honest and gritty. You may find that after writing it once, you need to go back and write it again because you just didn't quite get to the marrow of the bone. Like peeling back the layers of an onion, you may have to make a couple attempts before getting to the really good stuff.

Hopefully, the venting alone will make this exercise worth your while. You may even discover some new insights as you air your grievances. Now, however, we're going to ratchet things up a bit. This is where you get to practice your advanced Jedi moves.

From your letter, identify three of your issues – perhaps those that are the most painful or annoying, or the ones that tend to come up the most. List those three issues in your journal now. Taking Marjorie as an example, three of her issues might be 1) "He's so selfish"; 2) "He expects me to do everything"; and 3) "He's just so unkind."

Warning: The next step of this exercise may trigger you. It sure did trigger me when I first started this practice myself. To be fair, however, I'm going to make myself the sacrificial lamb here and use my own story as an example.

For the majority of my marriage, I saw myself as the victim of a hot-tempered husband who was dead set on controlling me. I had an arsenal of evidence locked and loaded to support this story, from disagreements about how much to tip at a restaurant to seemingly inexplicable outbursts directed at me in public. Because he was a fearless and powerful attorney who successfully took on Fortune 500 companies in his work, he was an easy scapegoat for my "poor, poor pitiful me" stories.

Then I found *The Work* of Byron Katie, and I couldn't play the victim anymore. As described in Chapter 5, *The Work* is a system of inquiry that allows you to explore whether the opposite of your beliefs might be true. The point is to get some mental relief. Namely, if you discover a painful thought might not actually be the truth set in stone, it's pretty liberating. In my case, I looked closely at my story that "I was the victim of a hot-tempered husband who was dead set on controlling me." Turned to its opposite, my original thought became "My husband was the victim of a hot-tempered wife who was dead set on controlling him." Could I find where that might have been true? Um, yes. Repeatedly.

Begrudgingly, I soon realized I was so obsessed with collecting evidence of my husband's bad temper and controlling tendencies, I'd glazed right over my own. For example, my husband typically got pretty worked up about frugality (which wasn't a natural tendency for me). I, on the other hand, was obsessed with how my husband presented himself to the world. I'd worry about his haircut, his belt, his shoes, his tie, or really anything about his appearance. And if he didn't acquiesce to my suggested changes, I would fume, sometimes overtly, and sometimes in the most passive of aggressive ways. I was absolutely dead set on controlling how he looked, and my temper would flare if I didn't get my way.

My righteous anger deflated a bit as I realized I wasn't as blameless as originally thought. And if I'd been able to poke a big hole in that particular belief, what other resentments was I holding that might not be so one-sidedly his fault? This exploration just snowballed. Suddenly, all those resentful angry thoughts became their opposite.

One of my favorite refrains, "He should care more," was particularly powerful when turned around. It became, "I should care more." At first, I bristled at the thought. Once I took a deep breath and looked below my holier-than-thou indignation, however, I saw something that hit me like a knife to the heart. Yeah, sure, there were places where he could have cared more. But when I got honest, like *really* honest, I had to admit to myself that there were so many places I hadn't cared about him beyond a superficial level.

Although we did not always speak the same love language, he loved me dearly and desired an intense emotional intimacy – one that I was either incapable of or unwilling to provide. I cared more about the shallow stuff, like our external appearances, both individually and as a couple, than I did about the foundational marital bond that was so important to him. If the roles were reversed, I'd be extremely hurt and damn angry, too. No wonder he was so irritated so much of the time.

With each turnaround, I chipped away at my "woe-is-me" story. I was no longer a victim but a co-creator in the misery, and I was genuinely sorry for my actions. What's more, looking at my flaws gave me greater compassion for his. It was like blowing back the leaves in the forest and seeing that trap on the dog's leg.

Take the frugality issue, for instance. It was not surprising that he had concerns. He had come from little and his astonishing success and wealth was hard-won. He knew the value of each dollar he'd earned. I, on the other hand, did not – as an only child in an upper middle class household, I hadn't worked for much by the time I got married. Until he pointed it out in frustration, I hadn't ever given my practice of over-tipping a second thought.

This example around tipping may seem trivial, but in most marriages where the vow is "till death do us part," the little stuff adds up. And as seen above, often the initial flash of anger masks a bigger issue hidden under the surface. You also may have heard before that our closest relationships are our greatest teachers. This is often the case because these people function as a mirror of sorts, showing us where we still need work or where we still need to heal. By turning my original statement around, I was able to look directly into that mirror and see my own flaws.

Now it's your turn. Remember those three big issues you picked from your Dirty Ugly Letter? I'd like you to rewrite those sentences in your journal, except this time, turn them around and substitute yourself in place of your husband. Then, follow each turnaround you write with at least one example to support it. See my samples below to get you started.

Original statement: He's just so unkind.

Turnaround: I am just so unkind.

Example:

I was unkind when I made a snide comment about my husband's mother last Thanksgiving.

Original statement: My husband watches too much TV when I'm around.

*****Now in this case, if you don't actually watch a lot of TV, think of something you do that might be an equivalent to his bad habit. *****

Turnaround: I spend too much time on social media when my husband is around.

Example: Last week, my husband tried to talk to me about something, but I blew him off to continue a comment war on Facebook.

And finally, for the cherry on top, we're going to blow the leaves away metaphorically, and see what the trap looks like below. Remember when I explained my husband's frugality? I want you to do the same for your beloved's transgressions. This is the part where we find a little compassion underneath the resentment. Running with the example above where your husband watches too much TV, why might he do such a thing? Perhaps it is because he works longer hours than he should and he doesn't practice good self-care. For him, mindless time in front of the TV is the only way he knows to shut off his mind and recharge a bit for the following day. In your journal, see if you can come up with some possible reasons (other than "he's just a big jerk!") for why he acts or speaks in the way he does.

For me, walking in my husband's shoes, as well as examining my own contributions to our conflict, opened up a wellspring of compassion that washed away many of my resentments, or at least allowed me to see my husband's perspective in a way that I never had before. And that exploration led to the final, most transformative step below.

Making Amends

It is likely that if you are reading this book, you are still married. Unfortunately for me, I didn't discover these tools until several years after my divorce. Regardless of which side you're on, however, this stuff works.

From Byron Katie's book *Loving What Is*, I was inspired to make amends with my ex by reporting on my role in our conflict and thanking him for the things he actually did well. I took all my big *aha* moments, like the realizations that I should have cared more, that I'd been controlling, and that I actually had a hot temper, and I told him about them.

I'll admit it: I really, really wanted to blame the heck out of him and protest that he started it all. I could have justified all of my behavior by pointing to his provocation or his original hot temper – but that's not what amends are about. I realize the idea of making amends may be as hard a pill to swallow as your spouse's affair with the hot nanny. Make no mistake, amends are not about condoning your ex's behavior; they are about freeing yourself through radical honesty.

Although I desperately wanted validation that my husband was the bad guy, I had a choice: Did I want to be right, or did I want to be free? Radical honesty is less about apologizing to your spouse for their benefit (although that can be a side effect of the process). It is, however, about cleaning your side of the street because it just feels good to have a clean street. Whether you stay or go, a clean conscience and a clean psyche will allow you to make decisions with more clarity and confidence.

In my case, I wrote my ex-husband a long letter owning my part, conveying my regrets, and expressing everything I appreciated about him. It was as healing for me to write as it was for him to read. Ultimately, it paved the way for constructive conversation followed by mutual apologies and even some laughter. That letter was the primary catalyst for our loving post-divorce friendship.

These days, I have my clients write this letter whether they are still married or are many years post-divorce. Now it is your turn. Dig deep, get radically honest, and put pen to paper. What part have you played in your relationship getting to its current state? For what do you feel bad? And what has your spouse done well, or for what are you most appreciative? What you do with this letter is up to you. However, by giving this letter to your spouse, you may be surprised with the goodness that can come back to you.

And one final note before you write this letter. This process is not about vomiting up anything and everything you have done so you can receive absolution from your husband. Again, this has little to do with your spouse and it has everything to do with owning the parts for which you want to take responsibility. You do not have to divulge every dirty secret you have. Only you know what is relevant and appropriate to share here.

The Cosmic Rewrite

My friend Sara Landon is an incredibly gifted spiritual teacher. A stunning blonde beauty, her bright blue eyes sparkle with joy and love as she shares her light with students and clients alike. Her work is a calling, and she is answering it in the most transformational of ways. But she wasn't always so happily tapped in, tuned in, and turned on to such a fulfilling existence.

Just a decade ago, Sara, much like me, had a seemingly perfect life. A high-paying corporate gig, a marriage to a good man, and an enviable life in the suburbs complete with a large house, expensive cars, exotic vacations, and plenty of money donated to charity every year. Then, in her late 20s, Sara was diagnosed with advanced stage, malignant melanoma. Over the course of the following year, Sara would undergo five painful surgeries and face her own mortality head on as her prognosis remained guarded.

Ultimately, Sara survived and has been cancer-free for years. Some might say it was a horrible tragedy that befell her at such a young age. Without her cancer journey, however, Sara may not have had the wakeup call that took her out of her old life and into the transformational work she does today. You see, despite the trappings of a perfect life, Sara had long suspected that she wasn't living her truth. Through her cancer, she was gifted a catalyst that prompted her to walk away from an unhappy marriage, work that was not meaningful, and a life that had left her wondering, "Is this all there is?" Without the cancer, she likely would not be living the authentic, fulfilling life she has today. By rewriting her narrative, the cancer that once seemed like a curse became a precious gift.

This practice of rewriting one's narrative to focus on the positives is a tool that I and many other coaches often use with clients. But it's a skill that doesn't generally come naturally to humans. In psychology, it's called the "negativity bias." According to Rick Hanson, PhD, a world-renowned psychologist, happiness researcher, and *New York Times* bestselling author, the negativity bias makes our brains "like Velcro for negative experiences but Teflon for positive ones." It is likely rooted in survival instincts, and it makes sense from an evolutionary perspective. Instead of remembering all the yummy berries consumed, for example, our brains will focus on the one poisonous berry that made us violently ill, thereby ensuring a better chance of survival in the future.

The good news is that the science of neuroplasticity has shown that we can rewire our brains. By examining our tired old stories and putting our fears up against inquiry, we can rewrite the narrative and create new neural pathways to support a life of greater happiness and well-being. Current grief recovery research backs this up, as well. Those individuals who can find meaning in a great loss fare better than those who don't. But rewriting our narrative and finding meaning in seemingly negative life events has many benefits beyond grief recovery.

For example, let's say a client (we'll call her Sue) lost her condo in foreclosure several years ago, and she is still experiencing a great deal of shame and grief around the incident. She identifies this as the worst thing that has happened to her, and she doubts she will ever fully recover. Sue also has an incredible rescue dog. Upon further inquiry, it turns out this dog was a stray that wandered up to the little farmhouse she was renting following the foreclosure.

Sue eventually had the dog certified to provide canine therapy in schools and hospitals. In fact, Sue ended up leaving a soul-sucking job she'd always hated to become an animal trainer who now certifies other rescue dogs for therapeutic work. She doesn't know what she would do without this dog and this work. But her old condo did not allow dogs. Without the foreclosure and subsequent move to a more rural area, she might never have found her true calling and her most favorite animal companion.

By rewriting the narrative of what she once believed to be the worst loss of her life, Sue realized that the apparent loss made possible her greatest joy. Perhaps you, too, can think of something good in your life that would not have been possible without a seemingly negative event. You've already had some practice in previous chapters by examining and rewriting your marriage story, as well as reframing your husband's faults. Now I want to take this practice to a new level and apply it to your marriage. We'll call this your Cosmic Rewrite.

Because we're ratcheting things up a bit with the Cosmic Rewrite, however, I want to preface this exercise with a little practice I learned from Martha Beck, who is a sociologist by training. It's called bracketing, and it is a social science method used by anthropologists where they temporarily suspend disbelief in order to study people and things that seem unbelievable. For example, a group of scientists is asked to study a community of people who believe they are direct descendants of Sasquatch. The scientists would put up an imaginary mental bracket and suspend judgment around the community's claims while they conduct their study. When their research is over, they would close the bracket and use logic and reason to analyze what they had observed. So, I invite you to put those brackets up now if you feel so inclined! And now, the Cosmic Rewrite.

Imagine if you will, that your Wise Authentic Self, or your soul, is eternal on the front and back end. It existed before this lifetime, and it will go on forever following your transition out of a human body. Your soul enjoys playing in the cosmos and it desires growth, expansion, and evolution. It looks for opportunities that will result in wisdom and increased empathy.

In much the same way an actor decides on their next role to play, your soul looks for variety and challenges, and it welcomes new experiences. So before you were born, your soul talked to a few other souls in the heavenly realm and came up with some ideas for what might happen once you all hit earth in human form.

Your soul goes on to pick its parents and life circumstances, like whether it will be born into poverty or wealth or somewhere in between. Like an actor evaluating a role, from a soul perspective, one is not better than the other, and both circumstances offer great room for growth. You might even choose some challenges you will face along the way, like a physical disability or loss of a friend. It's not a predetermined existence, but there are potentials that will exist for you to walk through (like a college major, declared and intended, but not set in stone).

One such potential might be marriage to a certain person. You agree in the heavenly realms with this soul that in your human lifetime you will meet and get married. You even ask them to up the ante a bit by behaving in a particularly difficult way or developing an addiction during the marriage you will have on Earth. From a soul level and in the eternal grand scheme of things, it actually sounds like an engaging challenge full of room for learning and growth, much like an actor selecting a particularly difficult role that will take them to their edge but grow them in their craft.

From this perspective, I want you to now think about your marriage. If the above scenario were true, why did you write your particular marriage to this specific husband into your script? What might you have wanted to learn? If you pull away to the 50,000-foot viewpoint on your life, what did you come here to experience on a soul level with this person? As your greatest teacher and mirror, why is this person in your life? Use your journal to record your answers.

From the perspective of your Cosmic Rewrite, what have you learned about your relationship? It's okay if this approach seems a bit far-fetched to you. Regardless, if you had to guess on the answers, what would they be? In the same way that a spiritual practice can provide perspective and resilience in tough times, a Cosmic Rewrite can help you find meaning and compassion in your relationship. Whether your marriage ends in reconciliation or dissolution, this shift in viewpoint can help you appreciate your relationship in terms of the soul adventure it was meant to be.

CHAPTER 11

Choosing Growth and Being the Change

One can choose to go back toward safety or forward toward growth. Growth must be chosen again and again; fear must be overcome again and again.

ABRAHAM MASLOW

You Don't Have to Leave, But You Can't Stay Here

At the Vancouver Peace Summit in 2009, the Dalai Lama said, "The world will be saved by the western woman." Many have speculated as to what his holiness meant by these words. I myself like to think his sentiments reflect a growing movement, especially in the West, toward female empowerment and an embrace of the divine feminine, full of fluid creativity and receptivity. It's my personal belief that we ladies in the Western world who are blessed with more freedom than women in more repressed countries have a responsibility to champion those

139

causes forgotten or ignored by the patriarchy and bring a new style of compassionate leadership to the forefront.

But here's the thing about changing the world (as so eloquently stated in a bumper-sticker slogan often attributed to Gandhi): *You must be the change you wish to see.* If we want to see more freedom, more compassion, and more courage, we gotta be practicing these things in our own lives. If you are living stagnant in an unhappy marriage, it is unlikely that you are living in alignment with your true being and up to your fullest potential.

At so many points throughout history (and even today in some countries around the world), marriages were entered based solely on caste, religious dictates, tribal survival, or financial or political motivations, such as transfer of wealth among the aristocracy. We, as those Western women the Dalai Lama spoke of, are blessed to choose our partners based on love and a desire to join forces with someone who lights us up inside. It is a *partnership*, after all.

At a bare minimum, your relationship should be energy neutral – it should not deplete you. At its best, your relationship should nourish and replenish you. It should provide you the support you need as you follow your calling and do the work in the world you came here to do, whether that means becoming an entrepreneur, raising great kiddos, speaking before the United Nations on social justice issues, or anything in between.

And let me clarify what I mean above. For example, if your spouse has a chronic and debilitating disease and you are the primary caretaker, of course that will require a great deal of energy and effort, but that's not what I'm talking about. Or if your husband loses his job or has an accident and needs some extra support for a period of time, again, that is not what I'm referring to. Or you hit a rough patch every now and then where things are tougher than normal in your relationship – that's not it either.

I'm talking strictly about things over which you have some semblance of control, such as how you relate to one another and communicate, how you get along, and your enjoyment of each other's company. Every relationship will have its peaks and valleys. If, however, your relationship lives in a valley year after year after year despite best efforts to get to a peak, *that* is what I'm talking about.

My relationship was not energy neutral. The constant bickering and fighting, added to the river of resentments already flowing between us, was incredibly draining. Often, merely being in each other's presence caused a physical response. I will never forget a cardiac stress test I underwent that my husband interrupted. I was already hooked up to the equipment that would monitor my heart, but I had not yet begun walking on the treadmill. When my husband walked into the examination room, my heart rate responded by immediately increasing substantially. Lest you think this was an anomaly, several years later I was lying in a recovery room after coming out of surgery, and my husband walked in to check on me. The previously slow beep of the heart monitor again increased considerably, prompting one of the nurses to come check on me.

That is what I'm talking about when I say a relationship is not energy neutral. Mine was quite literally creating stress just by virtue of being in close proximity with one another. And I was certainly no victim here – my mere presence often created a similar physical response in my husband, although we were not able to document it with an electrocardiogram reading. You may not have the benefit of heart monitor confirmation, either, but you know who you are if you suspect this could apply to you, too.

Staying in stagnation in an unhappy or wrong marriage has far-reaching effects, extending well beyond just your home life. For example, we now know that chronic stress impairs vital bodily functions (e.g., DNA replication) and thus accelerates aging. In our modern world, such stress often arises in situations where we feel trapped and helpless, such as a horrible job that nevertheless pays the bills, or ... a long-term relationship that provides security but makes you miserable. Did you realize a stressful, unhappy marriage could potentially take years off your life?

By remaining stuck – neither improving, changing, or leaving a bad relationship – you also are diverting vital energy and your precious life force away from where it is really needed, such as your purpose and calling. Just imagine what you could accomplish and the dreams you could take off the back burner if you weren't wasting your time, toil, and talent on marital discord and years of repeating the same unhealthy patterns and interactions. You don't necessarily have to leave your bad marriage, but something's gotta give. Something needs to change so that the majority of your life and energy are not devoted to maintaining the status quo of unhappiness and conflict at home.

What to Expect

And the time came when the risk to remain tight in a bud was more painful than the risk it took to blossom.
ANAÏS NIN

Getting out of stagnation and changing the status quo is big work. Well-worn behavior pattern ruts may be incredibly dysfunctional and unhealthy, but they are known and comfortable. Remember, our Small Selves (who are often running the show) resist change mightily and will come up with all kinds of reasons why change is not only impossible but downright dangerous. Yes, creating change carries with it a certain amount of risk. You cannot predict the outcome no matter how tight you are gripping the controls over your life. In the end, change was a risk I was willing to take – my pain of staying put had exceeded my fear of the unknown. If you are still reading, you may well be up for a bit of change yourself.

If so, congratulations on the self-awareness and honesty it takes to get to this point! Admitting this and making a commitment to change is just the beginning, however. Then it's time for the real work. In my own life, while the voice of my Wise Authentic Self has been steadfast in affirming my decision to leave my marriage, Ms. Holly (a.k.a. my Small Self) has had her fair share of freak-outs.

Knowing what to expect, however, can help you weather the storm. And having the right support along the way can make the sailing even smoother. Often, when the compost hits the fan, we forget the tools, techniques, and practices we've learned (such as those in this book), and return to familiar behavior patterns. Encouragement in implementation of the new patterns you are seeding and your new way of being is crucial. It's also easy to lose your footing and get caught in self-doubt, questioning your decisions and where to go next. Fortunately, I was blessed to have the help of a wonderful therapist, then later a coach, as I navigated the dissolution of my marriage. Their presence in my life during such a trying time was absolutely invaluable.

Compassionate witnesses in the form of supportive family, friends, and colleagues are amazing, too. However, after a certain period of time, these folks may grow weary of being your constant sounding board. In such cases, it might be time to enlist the help of a professional of some sort, in whatever form feels most appropriate and approachable for you. In the meantime, the following are some of the issues to be aware of and the pitfalls you may encounter along the way.

The Fear

After trusting your gut and listening to your Wise Authentic Self, you may know what you need to do, but are simply too afraid to actually do it. A couple things to remember when it comes to fear. No. 1, fear is simply part of the human experience. Some may have strengthened their tolerance for how much fear they can take, but fear is nevertheless part of the human package.

In fact, there is even a portion of our brain devoted specifically to broadcasting fear. Rooted deep down next to the brain stem, this particular area is called the reptile brain. At one point in our human evolution, it alerted us to saber tooth tigers and food scarcity. These days, it's still broadcasting 24/7, although the messages have shifted to more modern concerns, like running out of money or falling victim to a terrorist attack. Short of a lobotomy, this devoted brain center continues its constant broadcast of fear signals.

Although it may seem counter-intuitive, the best way to deal with a fearful mind is to accept it. You might have heard the saying that "what we resist persists." There is actually brain science to back up this phenomenon. So when fear arises, instead of attempting to push it away, acknowledge it and allow it to travel with you. As Elizabeth Gilbert recommends in her book *Big Magic*, give fear a seat in the car, just don't let it drive.

It's also helpful to remember that there are only two motivating factors behind human behavior: *love* and *fear*. If you are acting from a place of love, there is no room for fear. As you move forward, ask yourself whether love or fear is driving you. If it's fear, kindly request that your fear move to the backseat. Thank it for doing its job of trying to keep you safe – it is often just myopically focused on its one function. Love, on the other hand, sees the big picture. Love offers possibilities that fear does not. So put love in the driver's seat, and you will end up at a much better destination!

The Catalysts

When Katherine came to me, she knew she was in the wrong marriage. However, she wasn't quite ready to admit it to anyone else, including her husband. Our work together centered around helping her better own her truth about her marriage. For Katherine, this meant exploring a particular recurring dream she'd been having for the duration of her relationship. It was a particularly frightening dream for her, and it happened with some regularity.

In the dream, Katherine would find herself in a large, beautifully appointed house. Despite the house's beauty, Katherine knew there was something sinister lurking in its dark attic. She could approach the doorway, and at times dared to glance inside, but the darkness was so thick and foreboding, she'd rush back to a safe room on the main floor and attempt to avoid even the stairwell to the attic. As we analyzed her dream using a technique based on the work of Carl Jung, we discovered that the dark, scary attic was a metaphor for the places in her psyche she refused to acknowledge.

For many years, she had resisted the idea that she needed to leave her marriage. In the most benevolent of ways, it appeared that her subconscious was urging her to explore the idea that she was incredibly unhappy in her marriage. Through the recurring dream, it continued to nudge her to look at what was hidden behind that door. In the end, Katherine did leave her marriage.

During one of our final sessions together, Katherine happily confirmed that she no longer had the dream about the house with the scary, unexplored attic. She attributed this to finally listening to her Wise Authentic Self. She'd thrown open the attic door and took a hard look at the fact that her marriage was no longer working for her. After acting on this truth, it was as if her subconscious was able to let her sleep in peace.

You, too, may recognize a catalyst in your own life. I have had many a client who recognize the signs that something needs to change or that they are being called to take action around their marriage. Perhaps you have a recurring dream like Katherine. Or maybe you have a persistent bodily symptom when you're around your husband, like a stabbing pain in your gut. Or maybe your catalyst arrived in the form of strong intuition followed by some damning clues that your spouse is cheating on you.

Catalysts can arrive in many forms, both internally and externally. When they do, you have two choices: embrace them or ignore them. Ignoring them is often unsustainable. It's difficult to un-ring a bell once you've already heard its call. And like a toddler who's been ignored, these signs and messages often increase their volume and frequency until they are acknowledged. In my experience, it's better to lean into your catalysts. Allow them to speak to you, to convey the messages that you most need to hear. Often, it is the voice of your Wise Authentic Self begging you to listen so that it can lead you in the direction of your right life. So bravely embrace your catalysts, and let them move you forward.

The Soup

Tough life situations change the fabric of our very identity. They may be thrust upon you, like the death of a child or the loss of your entire life savings in a Ponzi scheme. Or you may knowingly and deliberately shake things up, like deciding to have a baby or make a mid-life career shift and go to medical school at age 45.

Whether you are the one doing the leaving or the one getting left, divorce is a huge identity-shifting change that will likely cause some turmoil in your life. Many spiritual teachers and coaches liken this change process to a caterpillar becoming a butterfly. I once thought that a caterpillar simply made a chrysalis and sprouted those colorful paper-thin wings straight out of his little caterpillar body. That is not at all what happens. Instead, it's an intense process whereby the caterpillar quite literally melts down into goo. From this caterpillar soup of cells, an entirely new organism is formed: a butterfly. It's a messy process in which the caterpillar lets go of who it was to become who it was meant to be.

In much the same way, when you get divorced, the married part of your identity melts away. Or perhaps it feels more like a painful death by fire. Either way, you are letting go of the old, and a new identity is forged. Your Small Self will likely cling madly to the old way. Small Selves do not typically welcome change. In the meantime, however, you become much like person soup. There are messy emotions, at times you may feel like you are dying, and you may have no idea what you are going to look like on the other side.

During this time, you will want to stay connected to your Wise Authentic Self, disbelieve painful stories that keep you stuck, feel all the feels, and practice good self-love and self-care (see Chapters

4 through 10 for a quick refresh). Following these steps will ensure that you are able to make it through the transition whole, emerge from your metaphoric chrysalis as a beautiful being, and embrace your new life with strength and ease.

The Unexpected Emotions

When Jill left her marriage, she was furious. Much like mine, her relationship had been filled with conflict and resentments, and her anger had fueled her departure. Any fear, sadness, or guilt never even had a chance to surface, as she tapped into her rage and past hurts. Those fiery emotions had her hurtling out the door at warp speed, with nothing but a glance behind her as she ran.

But Jill was now several years post-divorce. With space and time and some transformative personal work, most of her anger had dissipated. She'd made peace with many of the past hurts, and now, she was surprised to find an extreme sadness and guilt that she never expected to face. She still felt confident in her decision to leave, knowing it was the right one. But she couldn't help missing certain aspects of her life. And although her marriage had been conflict-ridden, her husband wasn't a bad man. She also noticed that peppered throughout her sadness were little bits of guilt – loose ends left untied with her former family-in-law, and things she could have done differently or better as she extricated herself from her old life.

So here Jill sat in my office, ready to embrace her new life but a bit caught off-guard about the tidal waves of sadness and guilt that overtook her from time to time now. Ignoring or resisting the waves seemed to make them worse, so Jill sought coaching to better understand and deal with these confusing emotions.

Having been in the exact same position myself, I was more than happy to help.

Over the course of our work together, Jill learned how to practice self-compassion and grace, as well as feel all the feels. By realizing that these emotions were normal, and by allowing them to crest and fall as needed, their frequency and intensity diminished over time. When I last spoke with Jill, she acknowledged the pain of her loss, but it did not carry the emotional charge it once did. She could remember the closed chapters of her life with fondness, while simultaneously welcoming a future full of possibility.

The Grief

Like Jill, you may be propelled out of your marriage by anger and resentment. Once the chaos and tumult of the divorce process comes to a close and the anger dissipates, however, you may come to a point where grief engulfs you. You may long for the familiarity and comfort of your old albeit dysfunctional life. This uncomfortable emotion does not mean you've made a mistake. It does not mean you should turn back. It simply means you are human. You are the caterpillar in the chrysalis, and this is something you must move through to become who you were meant to be.

Just as you have learned to feel all the feels earlier in this book, allow your grief to be there, even welcome it if you can. You may very well experience the kind of grief that makes it hard to breathe. Your heart may hurt terribly – it's no cliché, but a literal ache in your chest. You feel the urge to crawl out of your own skin. At times, it may be impossible to sit still – like your finite body cannot contain the intensity of the emotion.

Although it may be damn uncomfortable in the process, remember that our bodies and our psyches have a natural inclination toward healing. In the same way our cuts heal without us having to think about it, our psyches want to heal, too. By giving yourself room to process your sorrow, the natural resiliency of being human will pull you toward wholeness. Open yourself to this force of healing, and you may be astonished by how quickly your grief moves on through.

If All Else Fails...

When the going gets tough, you may want to turn back. This is normal – remember, your Small Self will resist uncomfortable changes with all its might, and this includes changes to your marriage, especially divorce. It wants to keep things predictable and safe. Be prepared for this by making a commitment to continue moving forward out of stagnation, whether that means big marital improvements or dissolution of the union. With every disappointment or setback or just plain old crappy day, allow yourself to cry, to rage, or to grieve. Give yourself space to feel whatever has come up. Then remember that this too shall pass.

For every step you take, the Universe will take many more. But that's the thing – you gotta at least take one step for the Universe to meet you halfway. You have to reach outward in order for someone or something to reach back. So keep the lines of communication with your Wise Authentic Self open to make sure you're headed in the right direction, and keep moving forward toward growth and change.

CHAPTER 12

A Graceful Divorce

A marriage can succeed as a soul adventure
even if it doesn't last forever.
MARTHA BECK

"Will the parties please approach the bench?" asked the judge, indicating she was ready to hear our case. As we made our way to the front of the crowded courtroom, I clasped my husband's hand in mine and tears began to well in my eyes. The judge was professional yet compassionate as she reviewed the file in our case, from our Divorce Petition all the way through to the Decree awaiting judicial approval. We were there that day to make our divorce final in the eyes of the law and the State of Texas.

We'd asked our attorneys to sit this one out. We wanted to approach this final step in our marriage the same way we'd approached our first steps as we walked down the aisle over ten years ago – with grace, intimacy, and intention. In much the same way we'd held hands in front of our minister as we recited our wedding vows, we held hands in front of the judge as she led us through the prove-up questions that outlined the terms of our divorce and made the dissolution of our marriage final. Tears rolled down our cheeks as we answered the judge's questions and our marriage drew to a close.

I'd spent my fair share of time in a courtroom as a law student and later as an attorney. This was, however, the first time I'd ever seen a court reporter cry. On our way out the door, we had a kind notary public take our photo to memorialize the occasion. Afterward, we headed to the Four Seasons Hotel for lunch. It only seemed appropriate to come full circle back to the same place where we'd been married 11 years prior on the beautiful rolling hotel lawn on the shores of Lady Bird Lake.

If You're Gonna Do It, Do It Gracefully

By now, dear reader, you may know how you wish to proceed with your marriage. You may have decided to stick around a bit longer and implement some of the tools in this book to improve your relationship. Or you may have reached the bedrock of your integrity and know that you know that you know that you need to end your marriage. If it's time for you to go, this chapter will serve as a guidebook to a graceful divorce. Divorce is not for the faint of heart, but it is for the strong of spirit. Your spirit is already inherently courageous and graceful – draw your strength from that eternal wellspring, and you will make it through like a champ.

Divorce: So Much More Than a Legal Proceeding

*There can be such a fear of hurting another or being the
contributing factor to someone else's despair that you
unknowingly stay in broken relationships, not seeing how the
most loving thing for both hearts is to go your own way.*
MATT KAHN, *Whatever Arises, Love That*

In my experience, once divorce is on the table and the parties are ready to initiate legal proceedings, the focus tends to shift toward getting the divorce finalized at whatever cost and as soon as possible. The parties usually just want the whole thing over with to get the pain behind them so they can move on. If you have attorneys involved, they will likely be doing their job by aggressively protecting your interests and keeping things moving at a fairly quick clip.

As the ball gets rolling, lines get drawn in the sand, and the battle is on. Paying attention to the mental, emotional, and spiritual pieces of divorce seems to fall by the wayside. Then you get through the proceedings, you have your decree in hand, the divorce is final, but there often is a wake of nuclear warfare leaving gaping wounds in you, your ex-spouse, and any other family or friends who've been affected by the process.

I'm not blaming attorneys or the legal system here – they are all functioning and doing what they were set up to do. But the legal system really wasn't designed to handle the emotional, mental, or spiritual elements of divorce. That's where I come in. Engaging a divorce coach or some sort of mental health professional familiar with the process can help you manage the parts that fall outside the jurisdiction of the law.

Much like a patient becoming proactive in their medical care, it will be up to you to decide how you want to handle your divorce. And your divorce is just that – *your* divorce, no one else's. Of course there is the legal component and the laws and guidelines you will be required to follow. But the rest of it is up to *you*. You get to write the rules. As you navigate the process, the following suggestions may help make it a bit more graceful.

Try a Structured Separation

One of the best pieces of advice I received during the tail end of my marriage came from my therapist who recommended a "structured separation." If you're still on the fence as to whether you're ready to end things, you might consider trying one. Although I had always viewed separation as a no-turning-back exit ramp with divorce as the inevitable destination, this was quite different. The parties go in with the intent that they may reconcile. They fashion specific rules, such as how long it will last, whether they will wear wedding rings, and how often they will see each other.

A dear friend who was ready to end her marriage did the equivalent of a structured separation for close to a year. Initially, she didn't have much hope of the marriage surviving. After nine months of profound personal work, however, she woke up one morning with a renewed faith in the relationship. They reconciled, and the marriage is going strong to this day.

This practice works especially well in high-conflict marriages. Why? Because when we experience large amounts of unrelenting conflict and trauma, our judgment can become impaired as our logical brain is hijacked by the limbic system. The result? Irrational, emotional decisions. When conflict is given a chance to dissipate, our logical thinking comes back online, allowing us to use our head instead of losing it. A structured separation provides a release in the pressure cooker created by warring spouses. You can then approach resolution or dissolution from a much more rational place.

Get Active

Divorce proceedings can leave even the strongest among us an angry shell of a person with nothing left to give. Still, try to be an active participant who isn't just carried along by the legal process. Studies show that cancer patients who are engaged in their treatment plan and healing fare much better than those who sit back and allow their medical team to dictate what will happen to them. Why not apply the same principles to your divorce? If your attorney proposes a well-intentioned or proven strategy that feels wrong to you, have the guts to say so. If you need more time to make a decision, request it. Remember, your attorney is working for *you*.

My ex-husband and I waited over a year to sign our Divorce Decree, despite the protestations of our respective attorneys. We held our ground. We knew we needed those extra months to let go gracefully so as not to leave a gaping hole of grief. You, too, can be assertive and write your own rules. Like a professional athlete visualizing a perfect performance, spend time envisioning how you want the proceedings to unfold and how you want your relationship with your soon-to-be ex to look.

You may not have a spouse who is willing to play nice. There were moments during my own divorce when tensions flared and I feared the worst. However, I found that by setting intentions, staying grounded, and doing visualizations of negotiations and my ideal future relationship with my ex, my energy affected my spouse's reactions and his willingness to engage constructively.

The opportunity arrives when you are in the midst of the proceedings and you decide consciously not to just go into autopilot and simply allow the legal process and your attorney to push you to the other side. For all those components that aren't merely legal (like the emotional, mental, spiritual, and even physical), this is your chance to work through some tough stuff instead of avoiding the pain (which will follow you!) and set yourself up for a positive new chapter once things are finalized.

If you can, remind yourself that the divorce is not happening *to* you – instead, you are an active and empowered participant. This might not feel so true if your spouse leaves and initiates divorce proceedings without much input. However, once this process has started, it's really up to you, regardless of the circumstances, to decide whether you will be a victim, or whether you will engage as a conscious co-creator and use this as an opportunity for tremendous growth, self-reflection, personal development, and maybe even an improved relationship with your spouse.

Avoid Nuclear War

Sometimes folks stay married out of fear of the court proceedings alone. But your divorce doesn't have to end in nuclear warfare in the courtroom. Did you know there are more peaceful alternatives, such as the Collaborative Law Model? There, all parties commit to resolving everything without going to court or even threatening to do so. The attorneys and other professionals involved (e.g., CPAs, financial planners, family therapists, and divorce and parenting coaches) are all trained in the collaborative approach and share the intent of keeping things civil and constructive. This is the model my husband and I used. In my current coaching practice, I work closely with the

Collaborative Law community and often encourage divorcing clients to consider this approach when it is appropriate.

It's not an option in all cases, though. Your spouse may be a rageful sociopath dead set on using nukes, making collaboration nearly impossible. While you can't control your spouse's actions, you can control your own energy and reactions. Instead of focusing on external circumstances, try bringing that focus inward. Take more time for self-care, much-needed rest, and connection to your inner wisdom through whatever means work best for you.

Author Janet Conner found herself in dangerous divorce where she feared for her life. In response, she grabbed a pen and begged for wisdom. As she channeled her pain and rage onto the page, she tapped into her inner guidance. Her writing helped carry her safely through her divorce, and ultimately led to her book, *Writing Down Your Soul*. Like Conner, you, too, have the opportunity to use your divorce to catalyze your own growth and create something beautiful.

Your Attorney Is Not a Weapon

Another pitfall to avoid is using your attorney as a weapon to do and say the things that for whatever reason you either didn't or couldn't say during your marriage. I myself was guilty of this at one point. Although I ended up selecting an incredibly well-respected older male attorney known for his even-keel professionalism, my initial inclination was to engage a female attorney with quite the reputation among the family law bar in Austin. She was known as a bit of a ball-buster, and while I still adore her as a person, hiring her conveyed a very clear message as to how the proceedings would go down (read: scorched earth following nuclear war). As mad as I was at my husband and as powerless as I felt in the marriage, I locked onto her as my saving grace and envisioned her standing up for me and conveying just how pissed I was.

I should have known better – my husband heard me mention her once, and the entire energy around the process changed. Without him ever uttering the words, his look said, "Oh, so that's how you're going to play? Duly noted. Let's lawyer up and get ready for WWIII." Fortunately, this crisis was averted, as I ultimately chose a more sensible attorney for our circumstances. But it meant I had to show up and talk to my husband about some hard stuff instead of hiding behind an attorney and hoping how she handled my side of the case would make my husband understand how hurt and angry I was.

Instead, I mustered my courage, got radically honest, took responsibility for my part, and made amends as best I could. My attorney served not as a shield or a guard, but as what he was designed to be – an expert in family law whose job was to simply guide me through the legal process. It was up to me to write the rules of my own personal conduct, process my tough emotions, and lean in for the spiritual growth that became possible when I showed up and did the transformational personal work.

The Importance of Ritual and Ceremony

Chances are, you put at least a little bit of thought and planning into your wedding. You and your beloved likely selected the people you wanted to be surrounded by, the clothes you would wear, the vows you would recite, and any other elements that were special and meaningful to you.

For humans, ritual and ceremony are important. They provide touchstones during a lifetime and honor significant transitions. Unlike the care and preparation given to a wedding, however, divorce unfortunately usually receives short shrift. The parties are typically in so much pain that they avoid any acknowledgement of the process, much less a celebration of it. In much the same way as a memorial service, however, a ceremony around your divorce can be a very healing process.

Depending on how contentious things are, you may be the only one doing this ceremony. It doesn't have to be big. It simply needs to be meaningful. For my ex and I, that meant doing the final steps of our divorce together, without our attorneys present. We wanted to look each other in the eye and honor what we'd done well, kind-of an undoing of our vows, or a reimaging of them. For you, that may mean selecting some photos or mementos from the marriage and burning them ceremoniously as an effigy in your backyard. Or going to your favorite river or body of water and performing a cleansing akin to a baptism into your new single life. Or holding a divorce party, similar to a wedding reception, where friends and family can support one or both of you as you enter into the next chapter of your life.

Again, you write the rules here. Simply ask yourself what you need to feel whole and complete around the process. How can you best honor the past and embrace your future? Whatever that looks like for you is perfect – like your wedding, it should reflect your unique desires and intentions, whatever those are.

Look Out! Reconciliation Possible

You may find, as I did, that after walking through all the steps in this book, from getting connected to your Wise Authentic Self, to examining your painful thoughts, to getting radically honest about your role in your marriage – you have more compassion for your husband and greater perspective about your conflicts and resentments. There was a point for me along the way where reconciliation was entirely possible had we wished it to be so. Although ultimately I decided that my best life was not with my awesome ex-husband, the anger and resentment had almost completely dissipated, the slate between us had been wiped almost completely clean, and we had a new appreciation and fondness for each other that had never existed while we were together. You may get to this point before ever leaving your marriage.

That is my hope for you, dear reader – not that you get divorced (although I fully support an informed decision to go this route!), but that you do the work to get to a place where you can evaluate your marriage from absolute clarity, peace, and courageous action. Then, if you do decide that dissolution is necessary, you can do so fearlessly, with great wisdom, grace, and love.

CONCLUSION

I hope you live a life you're proud of. If you find that you are
not, I hope you find the strength to start all over again.
ERIC ROTH, *The Curious Case of Benjamin Button*

We've covered a lot of ground in our time together. From connecting to the guidance of your Wise Authentic Self, to identifying a marriage story that works for you, to feeling all the feels and embracing self-love, all the way to spirituality, radical honesty, and even graceful divorce – congratulations on hanging in there!

There are so many ways to remain stagnant in our lives, whether it be in a job we hate, a health condition we ignore, an addiction that goes untreated, or, as we've covered here, a marriage that stays stuck in dysfunction and conflict indefinitely. I am passionate about helping others get out of mucky stagnation, and my specialty as a coach (because it was my own Hell and back) is helping women get unstuck from their bad marriages.

By now, you may have realized that getting unstuck doesn't necessarily mean you must leave your marriage. The stories and tools in this book can help transform you and your relationship such that divorce may no longer be your first choice. But it's also okay if it is. Whatever you decide, I honor that choice, knowing that whether to remain in a marriage is an acutely personal decision. While your decision is not my business, helping you make an informed one in alignment with your personal truth is.

Also, know that any suffering you are experiencing can be seen as a call to awaken – awaken to a new way of being such that we change our lives and, in turn, the world. It may seem like it's just you in this painful place going it alone. However, know that this evaluation of your relationship plays an important role in the larger tapestry. By looking at your unhappy relationship, you are lighting the way for others to do the same and to step into their own truth. This is your chance to step into the life you were meant to live and the potential that you came here with – the life lived in a white light blaze of glory!

No matter what you decide, I wish for you not only the courage and clarity to move forward in a way that honors the deepest desires of your heart and spirit, but also the expansion into a new life that you love.

ACKNOWLEDGMENTS

You can't connect the dots looking forward; you can only connect them looking backwards. So you have to trust that the dots will somehow connect in your future. You have to trust in something – your gut, destiny, life, karma, whatever. This approach has never let me down and it has made all the difference in my life.

STEVE JOBS

The road to writing this book has been long and winding. Looking backwards now, the dots have connected so beautifully. Like the magical helpers and mentors who arrive on the hero's path in Joseph Campbell's *The Hero With a Thousand Faces*, many of the most important dots in my life are incredible, loving people who serendipitously appeared and assisted me along my way.

To Martha Beck, whose writing was my cosmic alarm clock. Thank you for your wit, wisdom, honesty, and authenticity. Your writing helped me recognize I was living a life that was not my own.

To Kumara Wilcoxon, whose friendship, fun, and love served as the most potent catalyst for my awakening. Thanks for being such an integral part of my soul family. And to Leslie

Scofield (a.k.a. Sco), whose constant joy and unending support helped me see there was a book in my story.

To Chase Buttice, who reminded me it's never too late to meet an amazing girlfriend in a new city. As if hours upon hours of hashing through the big issues over many glasses of wine wasn't enough, thank you for so graciously sharing with me your gift of healing touch – it kept me going through some of the darker parts of this process.

To Stephanie Levenston and Ariel Hubbard, whose intuitive gifts and energetic healing were absolutely invaluable over the last year. My sessions with you all were like oases in a desert – it is no exaggeration to say I would not have made it through without you both!

To Tara Daniels, whose weekly accountabilibuddy role has turned into one of the most meaningful friendships I could have ever imagined. Thank you for sticking around after your near-death experience; thank you for bringing so much magic back from the other side; thank you for sharing your angelic presence with us all; and thank you for holding such peaceful space – you have kept me sane when I've been about ready to drop my basket.

To my most amazing clients, whose stories have shaped my work and transformed my life.

To all the entities seen and unseen, known and unknown, whose love, light, guidance, and assistance come straight from the Divine to help us humans on our way.

To Angela Lauria, whose vision and mentorship has been a beacon for the last several years of my life. Thank you for boldly going where you've gone, and bringing us along with you. Without you, my first book would never have happened this soon.

To the Morgan James Publishing team: Special thanks to David Hancock, CEO & Founder for believing in me and my message. To my Author Relations Manager, Tiffany Gibson, thanks for making the process seamless and easy. Many more thanks to everyone else, but especially Jim Howard, Bethany Marshall, and Nickcole Watkins.

To my Mom & Dad, whose steadfast support and love have remained constant my entire life. Thank you for giving me a name that I've loved growing into. Thank you for remaining curious, even when that isn't always the easiest choice. Thank you for believing in my ability to be the best at whatever my heart leads me to pursue.

And to the two most amazing men in the world – how I've been blessed enough to have you both in my life is beyond me...

First, to Rob, without whom I would not be where I am today. You challenged me, grew me, humored me, protected me, and loved me so intensely in your most unique of ways. Thank you for the life that you provided for us – it was beyond my wildest dreams. Thank you for showing me what it looks like to be comfortable in your own skin. Thank you for doing forgiveness with me and making amends – you certainly didn't have to, but what a freaking gift! Thank you for your continued presence in my life. I can't wait to debrief on the other side – and for you to confirm I was right about this whole afterlife business!

And finally, to Chase, the love of my life who followed a wolverine from Seattle to Austin to find me and bring me home, literally and metaphorically. Your gentle, peaceful love healed me from the inside out. Thank you for being my biggest cheerleader and for having the patience of Job while I finally found my way in business and life. Thank you for not being crazy on the same days I am. Thank you for making me laugh *so damned much*! Thank you for creating the happiest of homes and lives with me – I can't wait for the adventures to come!

ABOUT THE AUTHOR

Sunny Joy McMillan is a recovering attorney and a practicing master life coach who did her coach training and certification through Dr. Martha Beck's program. She hosts "Sunny in Seattle," a weekly radio show that airs on Fridays from 9 – 10 a.m. Pacific on Alternative Talk 1150AM KKNW where she interviews inspiring guests like Byron Katie, Neale Donald Walsch, Mark Nepo, and more. She's also a happy divorcée who, after a high-conflict marriage, shared a loving post-divorce friendship with her ex-husband until his passing in 2018. Sunny is passionate about empowering adults to make soul-based relationship choices, as well as using divorce as a catalyst for personal transformation, spiritual awakening, and creating an awesome new life. She works with individuals and groups through her coaching practice in the University District of Seattle.

Website: www.goldenoversoul.com
Email: sunnyjoy@goldenoversoul.com

Want more
Unhitched goodness?

Get personalized video training
on getting clear about your
marriage, gaining courage
to make tough decisions, and
creating hope for a
bright future at:

www.unhitchedbook.com

THANK YOU

Thank you for reading Unhitched!

By Sunny Joy McMillan

Attorney + Master Life Coach

Morgan James makes all of our titles available
through the Library for All Charity Organization.

www.LibraryForAll.org

Printed in the USA
CPSIA information can be obtained
at www.ICGtesting.com
JSHW022341140824
68134JS00019B/1614